"Innate Subtlety"

An Exploration of Creation

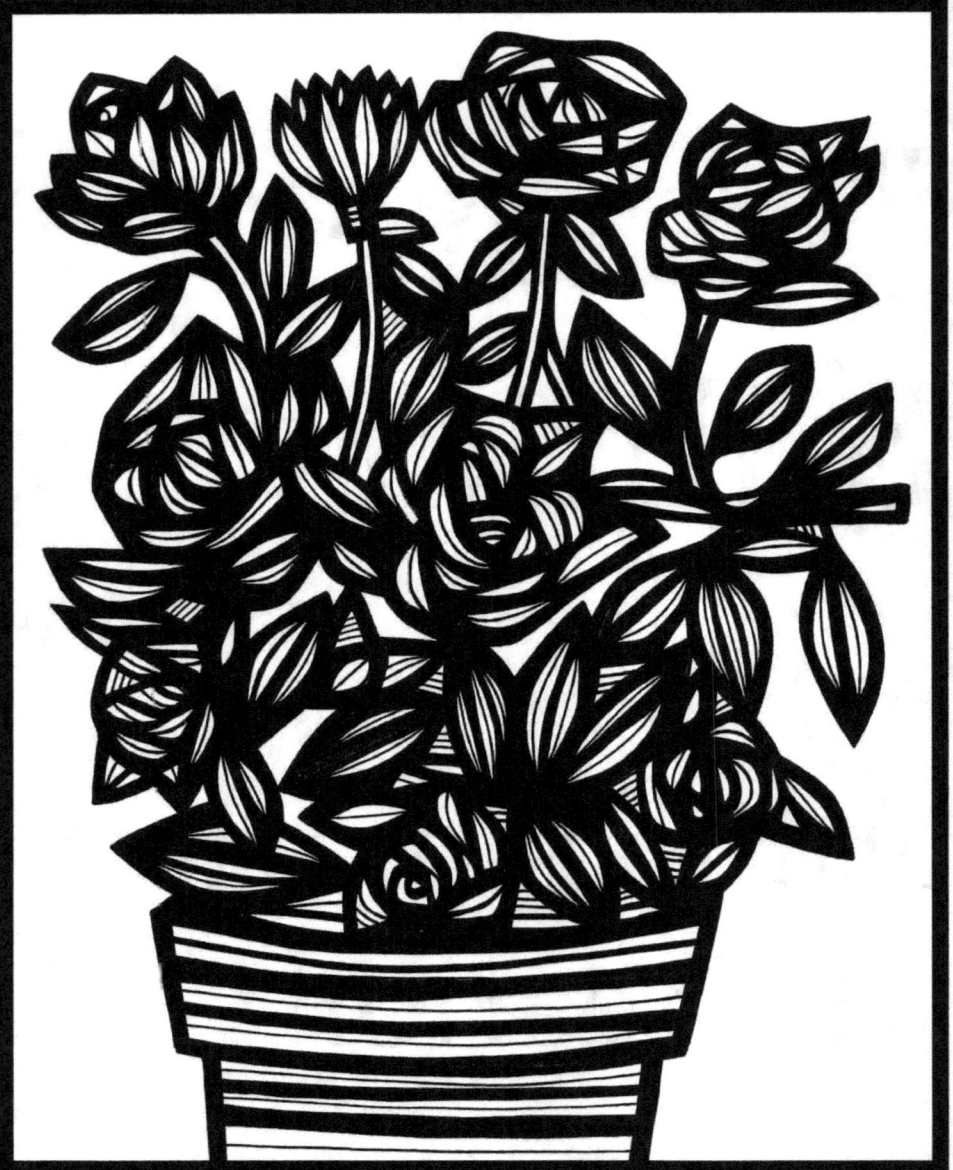

Words by:

Zbigniew Zolkowski

and

Eddie Alfaro

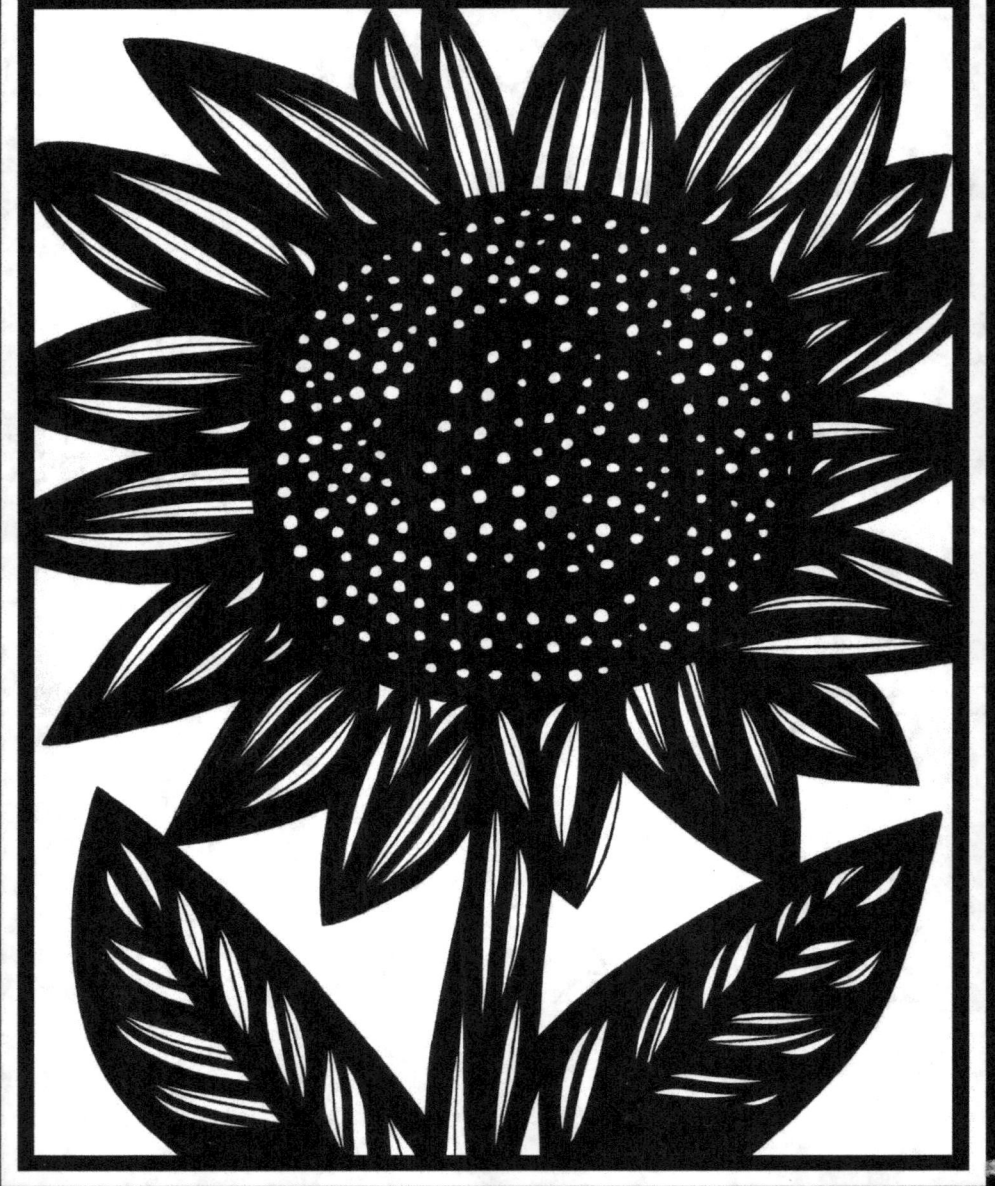

Artwork by:

Eddie Alfaro

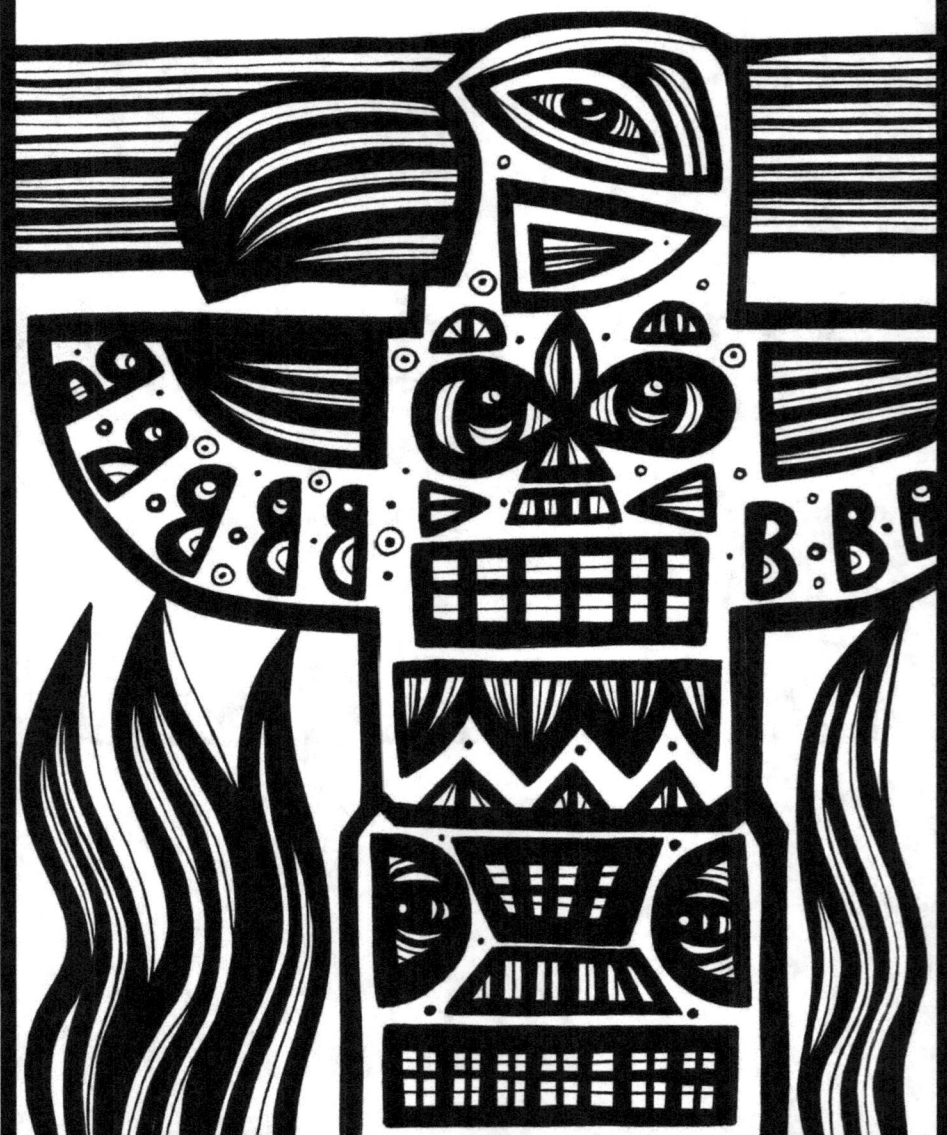

"Genesis of the Explosion"

by Eddie Alfaro

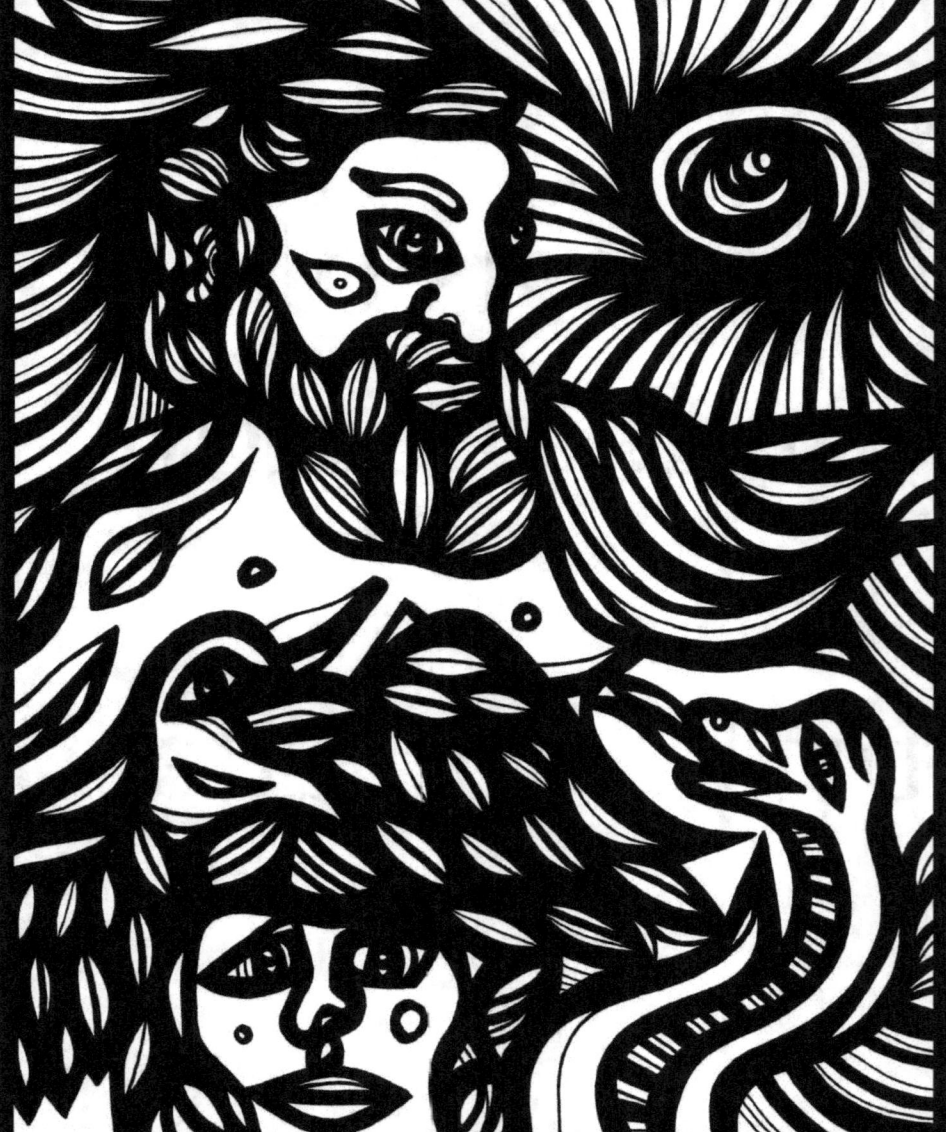

The beginning
is the seed,

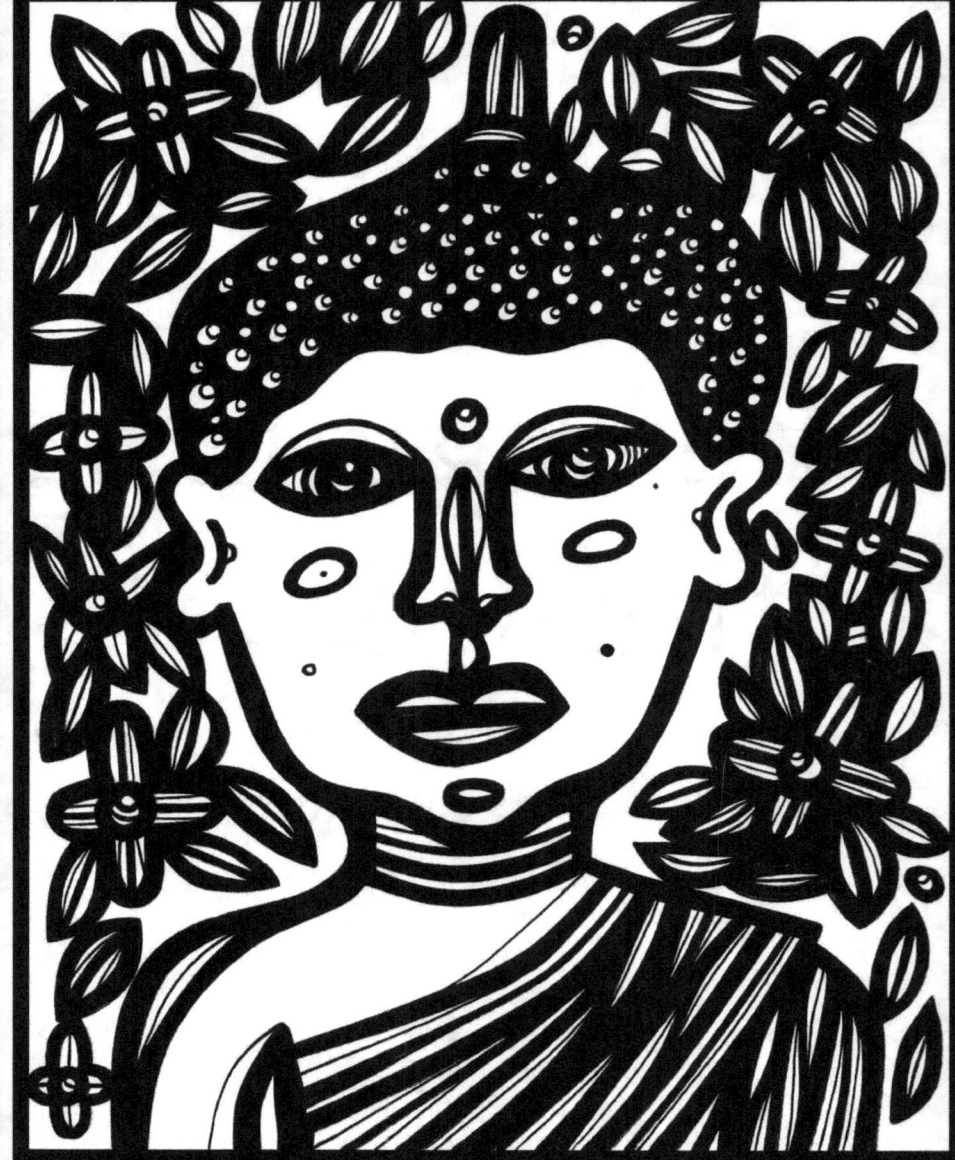

The born again, not to be seen but felt, feeling of birth.

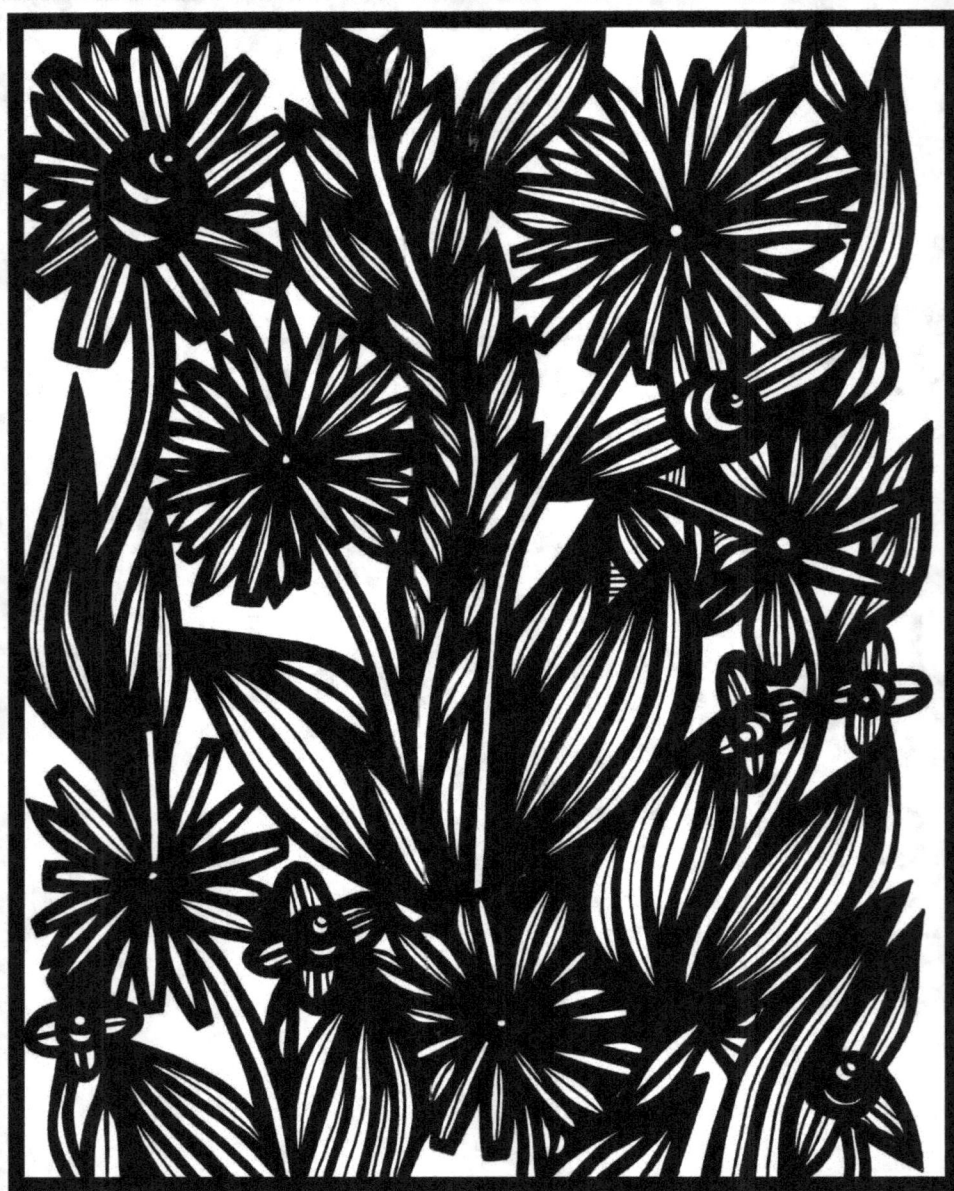

A dream, a moment of creation.

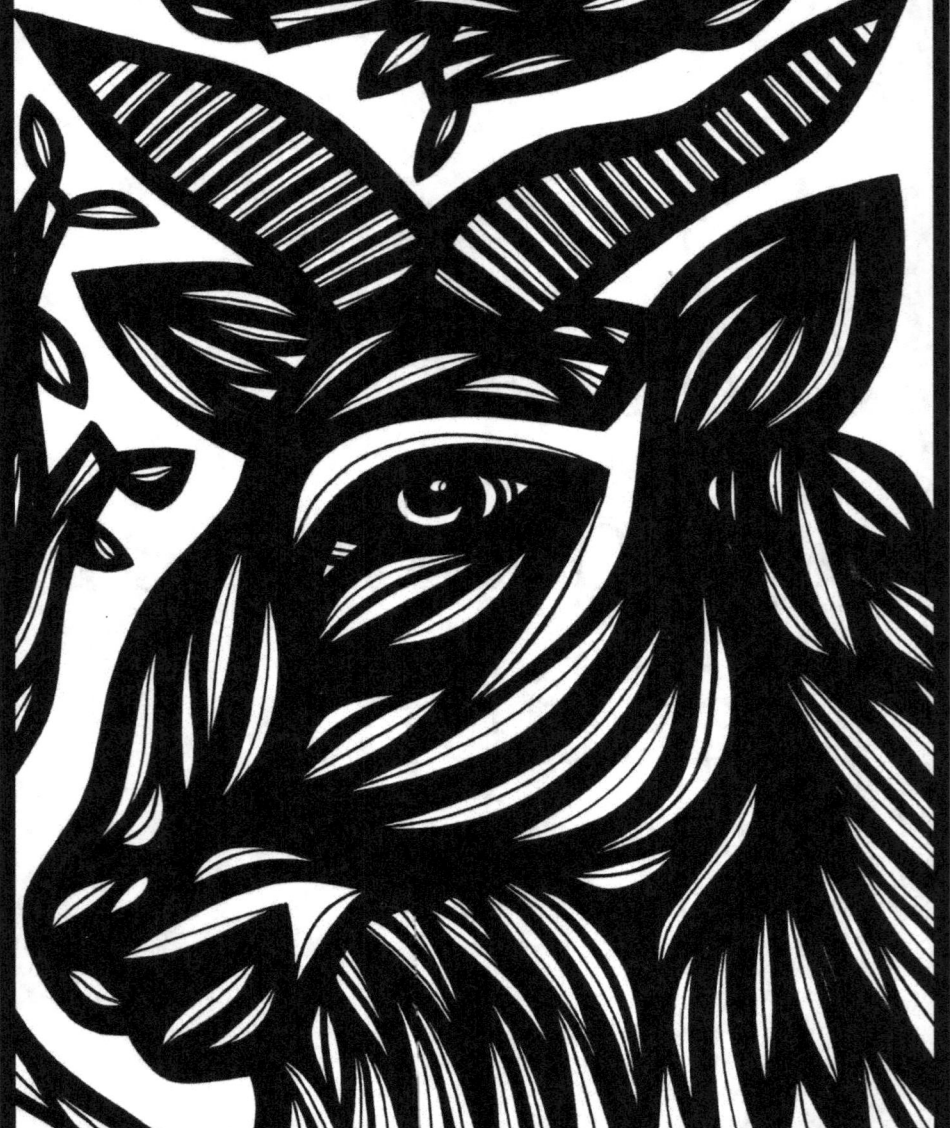

The genesis of the explosion!!!

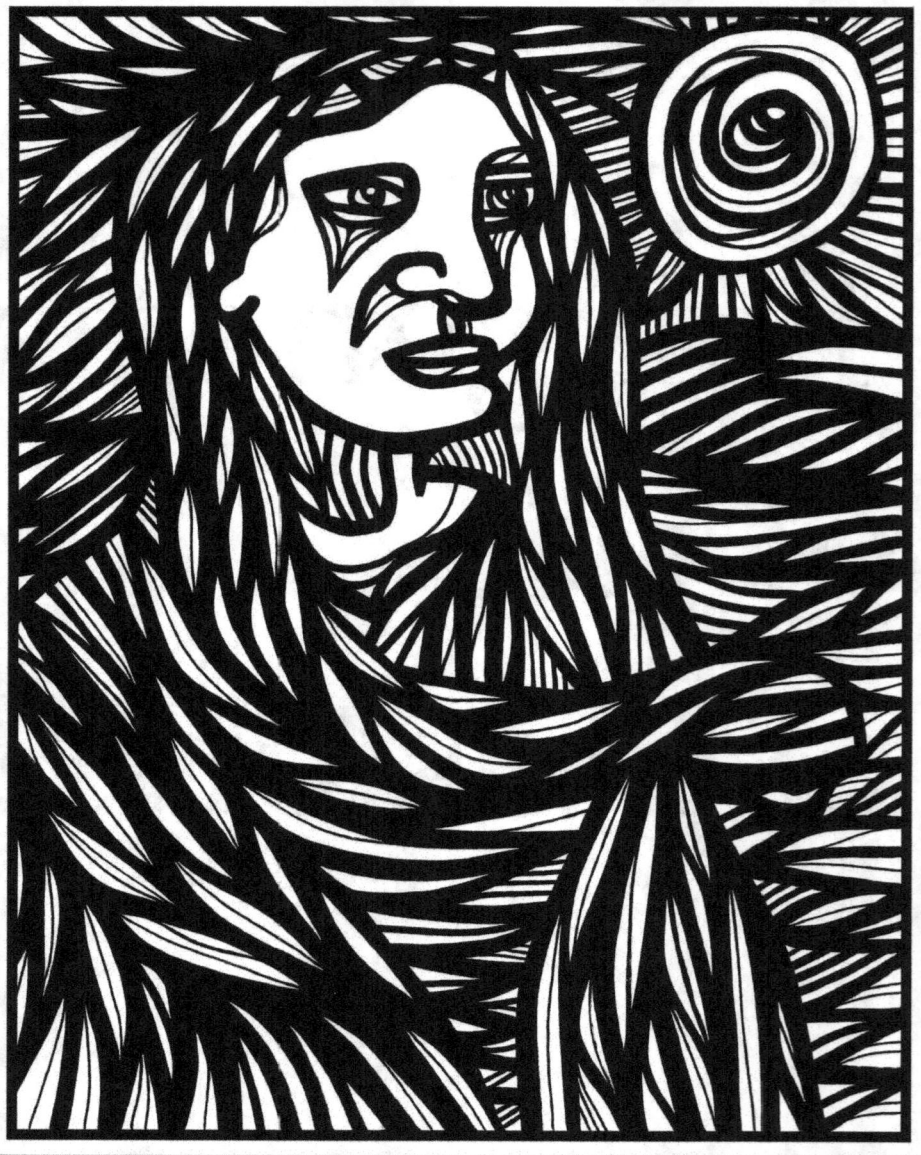

A time to see,
and say a word,
about how things
are made.

A sentence to say,
the energy
of a growth.

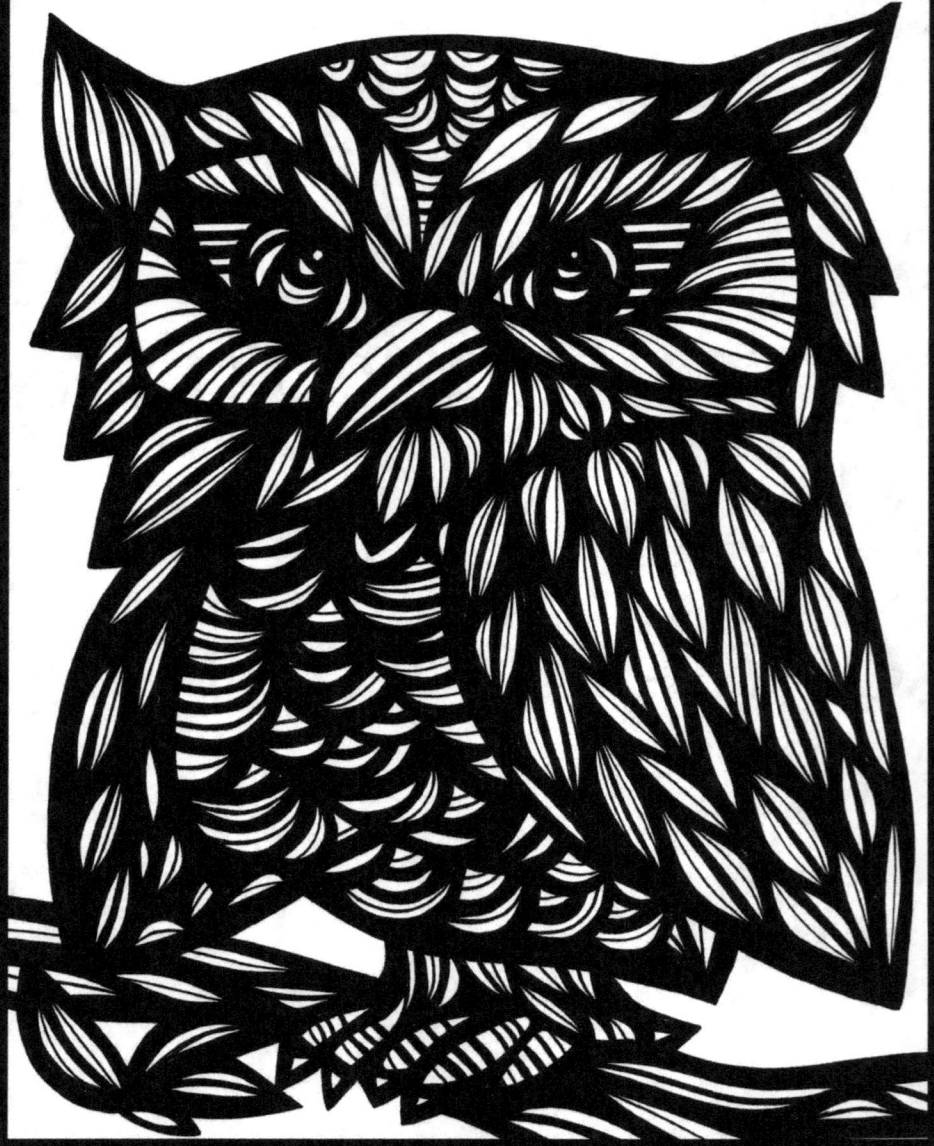

A bold start to the time of an organism.

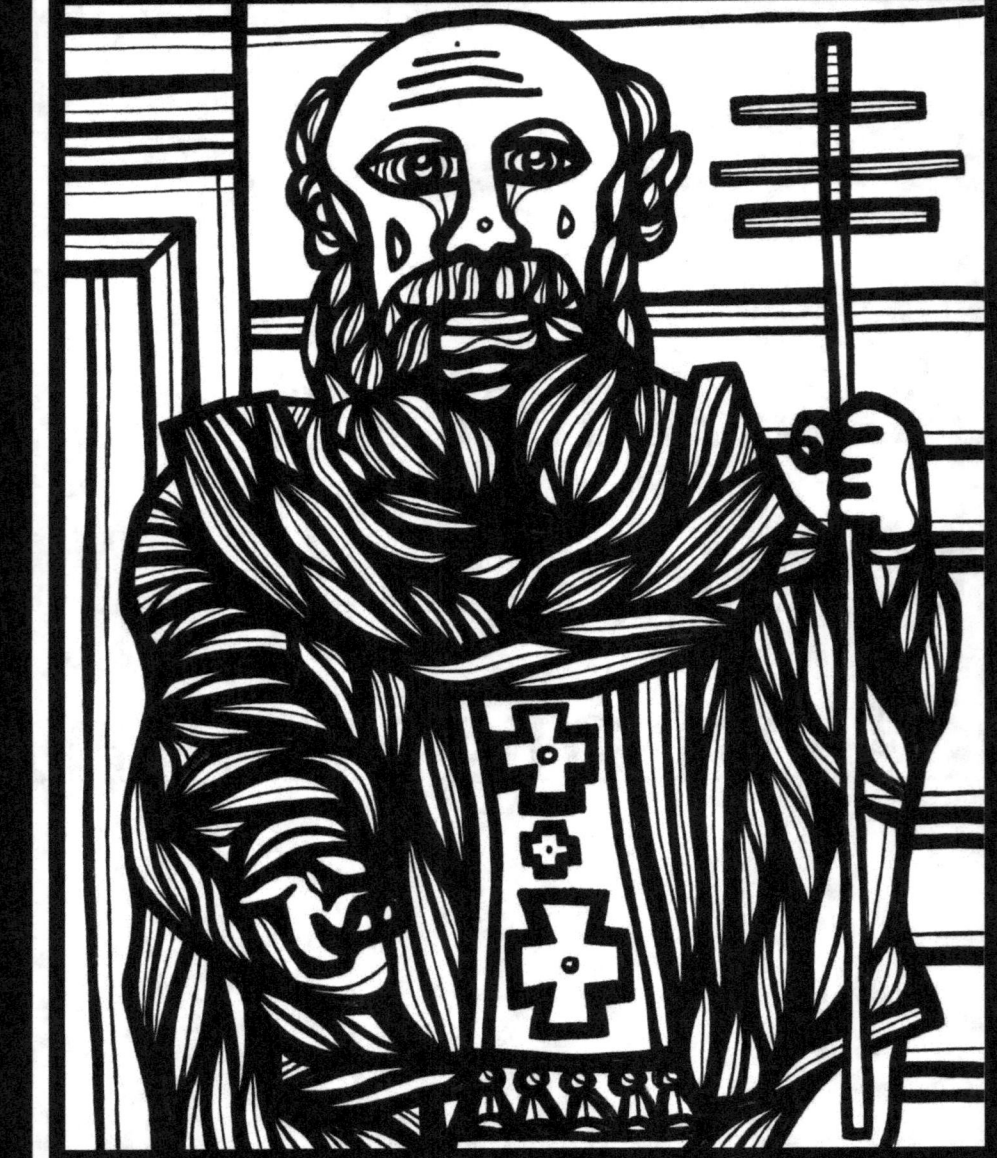

Destruction in an opposite form.

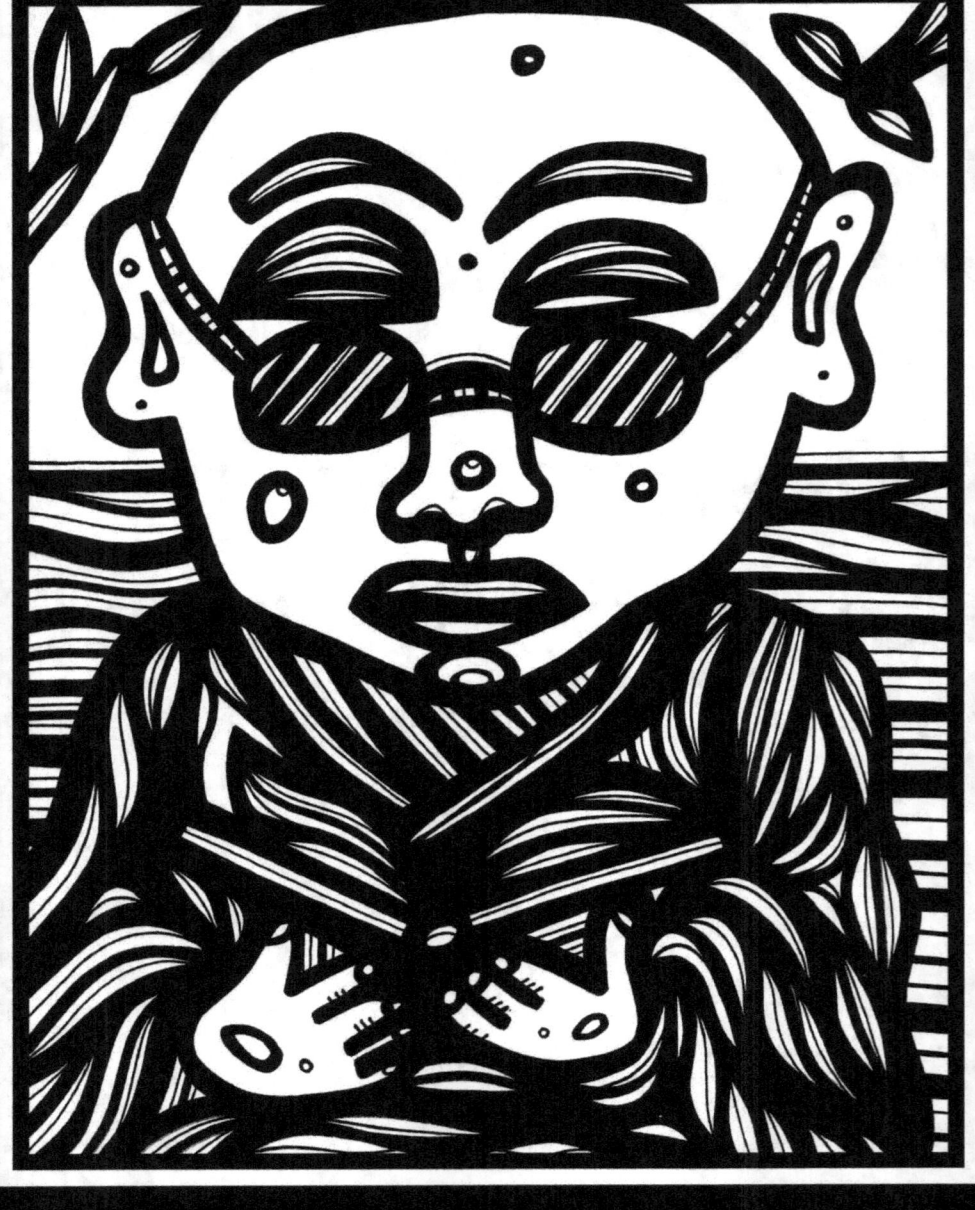

The construction of
a lifetime.

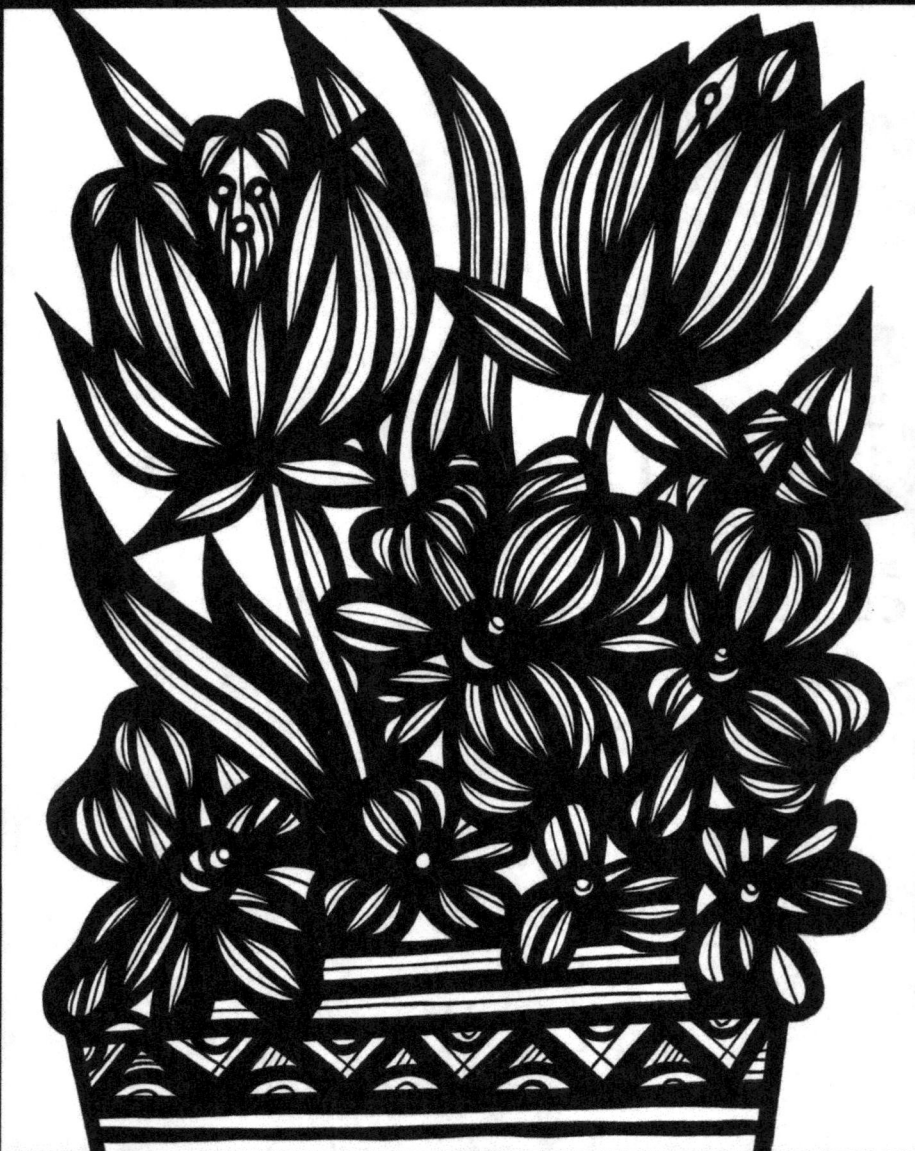

"Seeds That He Placed in the Living Earth"

by

Zbigniew Zolkowski

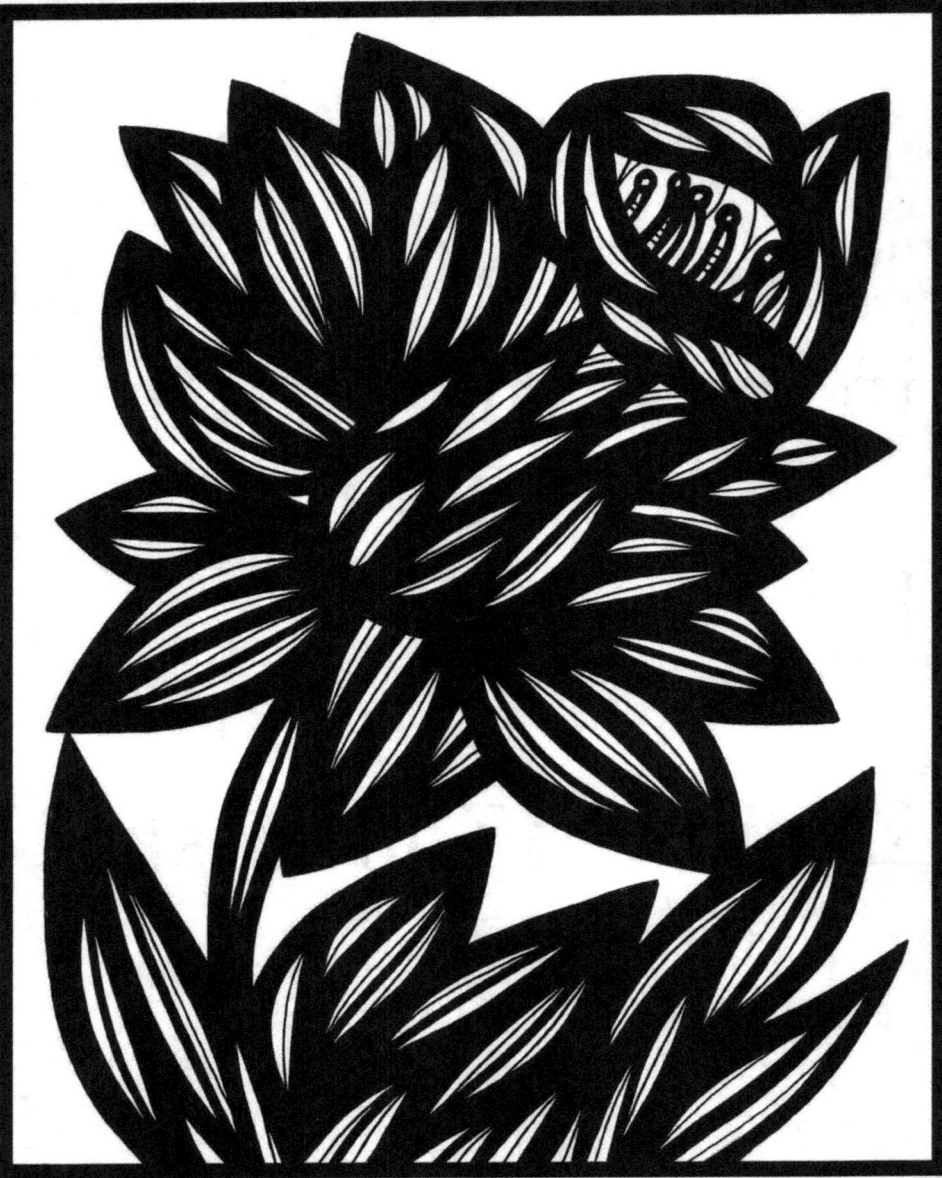

Saint Francis often conversed with animals, with flowers.

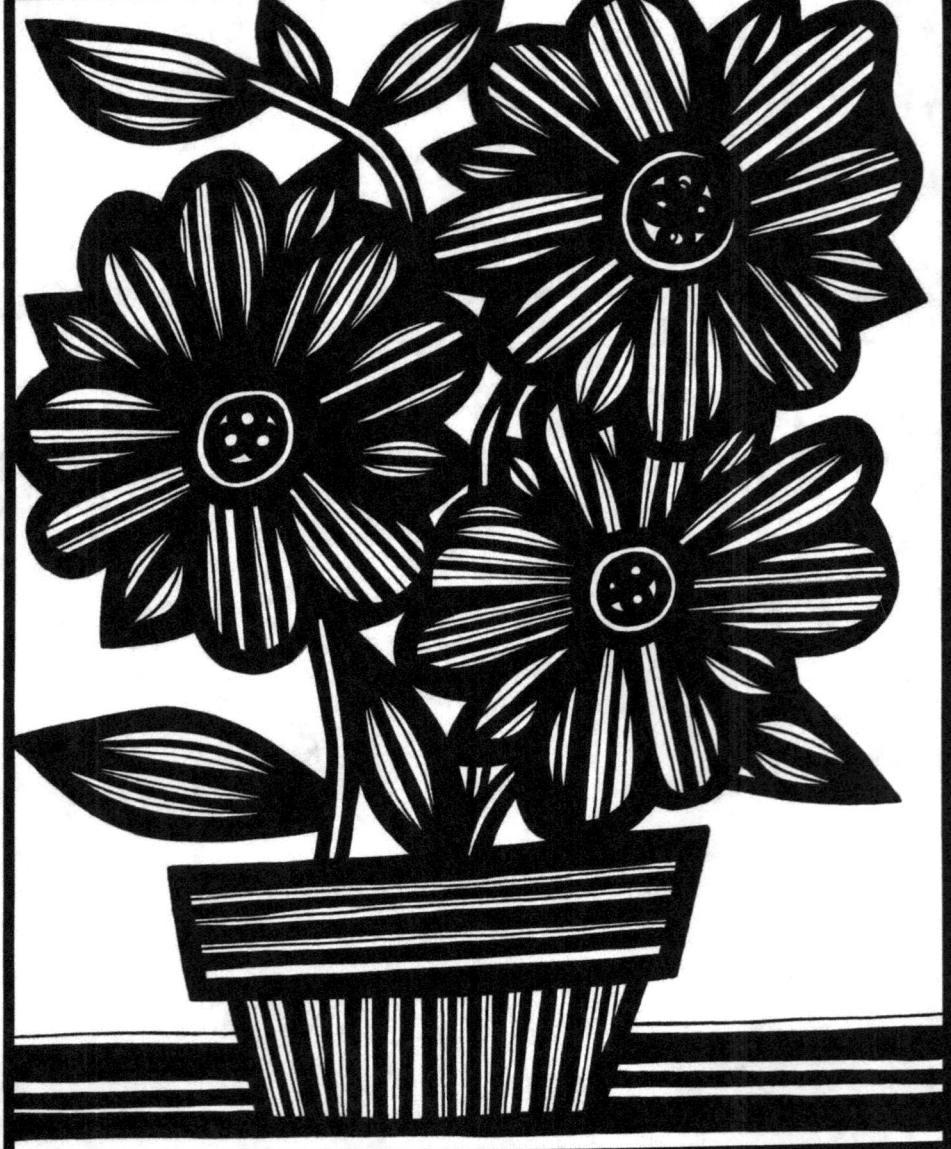

He conversed,
while he prayed,
while he danced,
while he played
and worked.

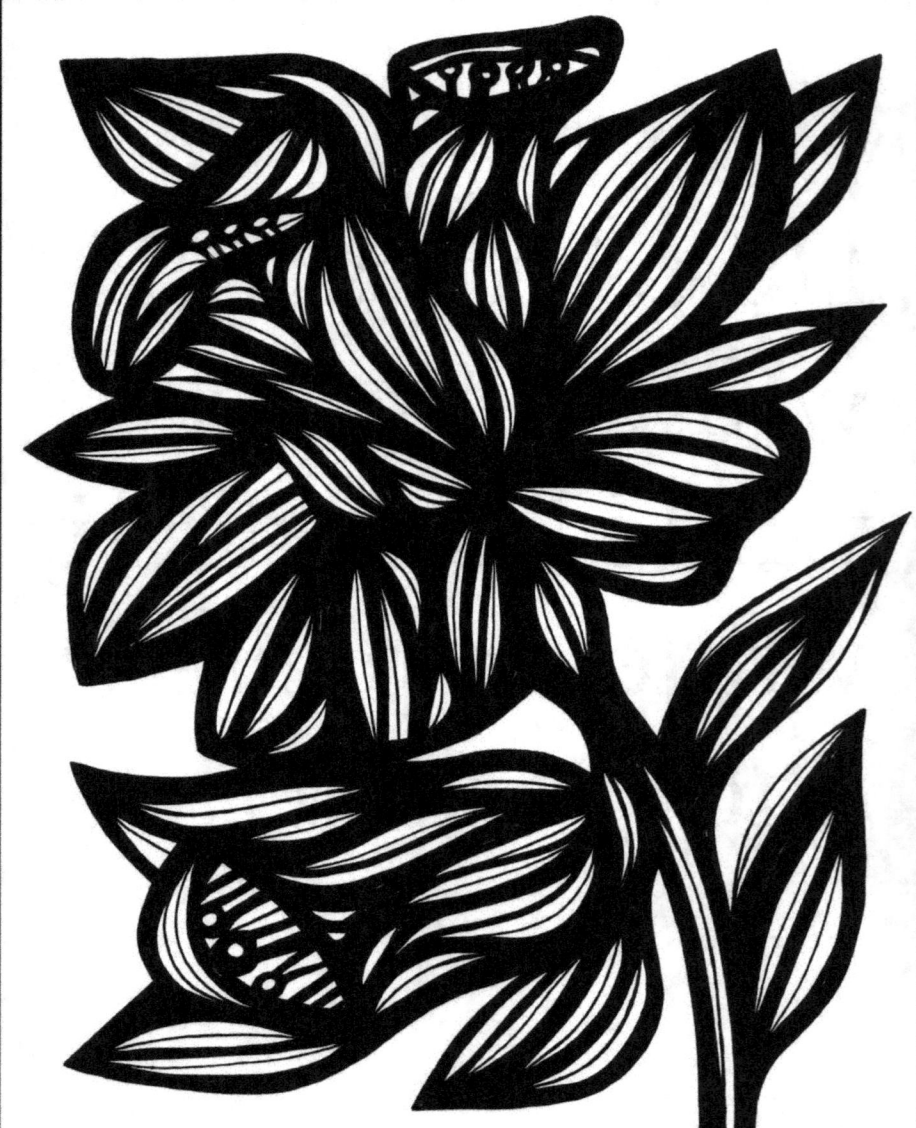

He sang with them
all this lovely songs,

He had no thought
of making any distinction
between anything which
God placed upon this earth.

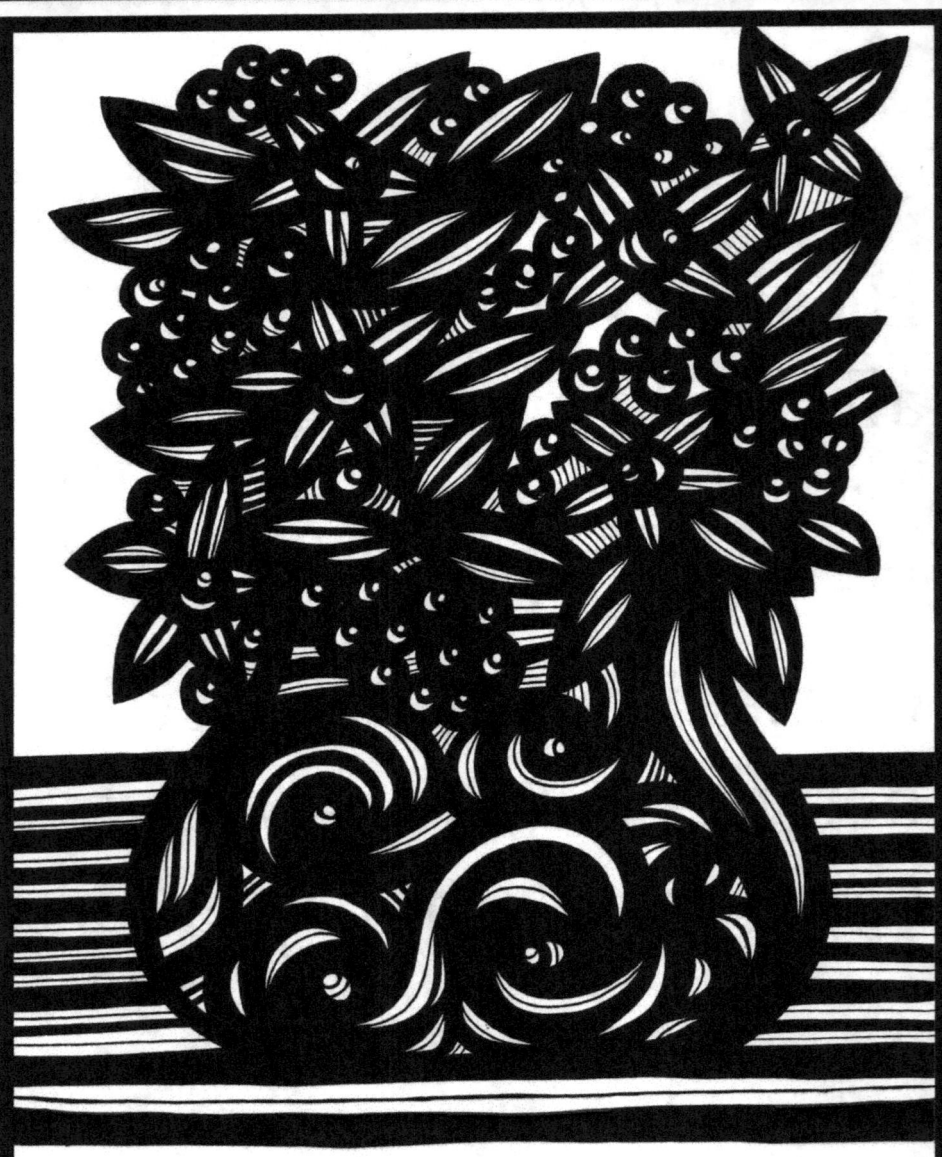

Saint Francis gave away everything that he made with his hands.

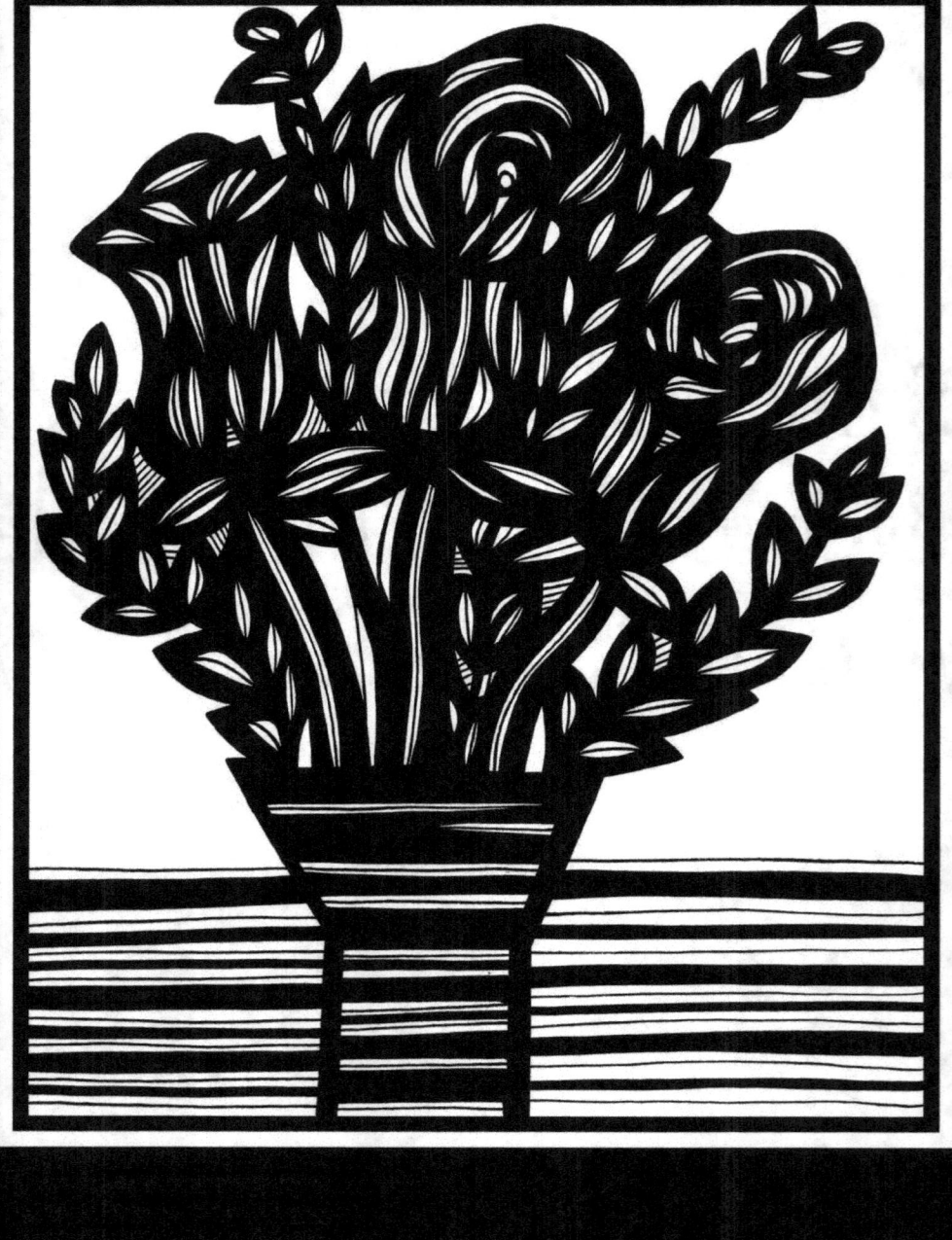

For even his prayers had wings like doves.

Free like all living things like seed that he placed in the living earth.

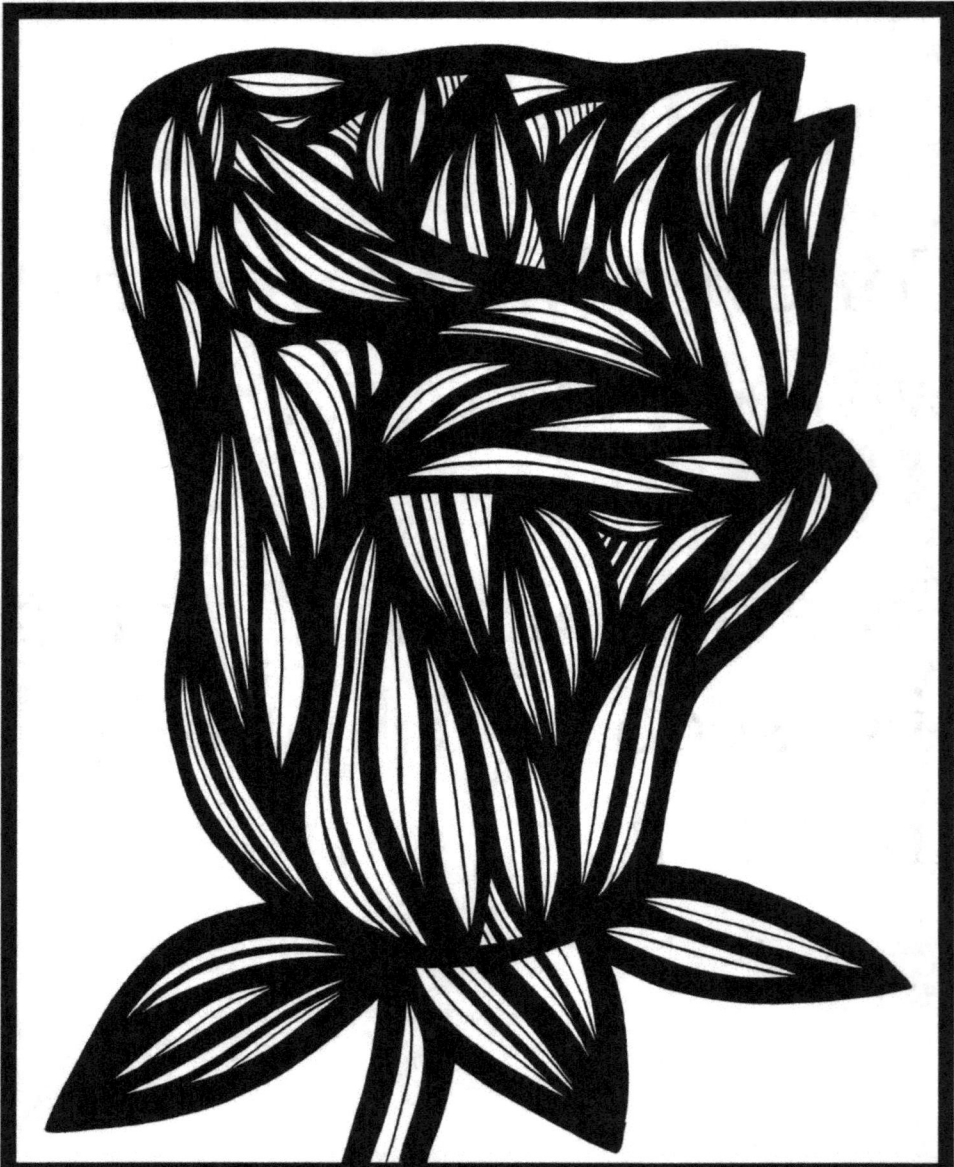

All his thoughts, centered on love that enveloped everything he touched.

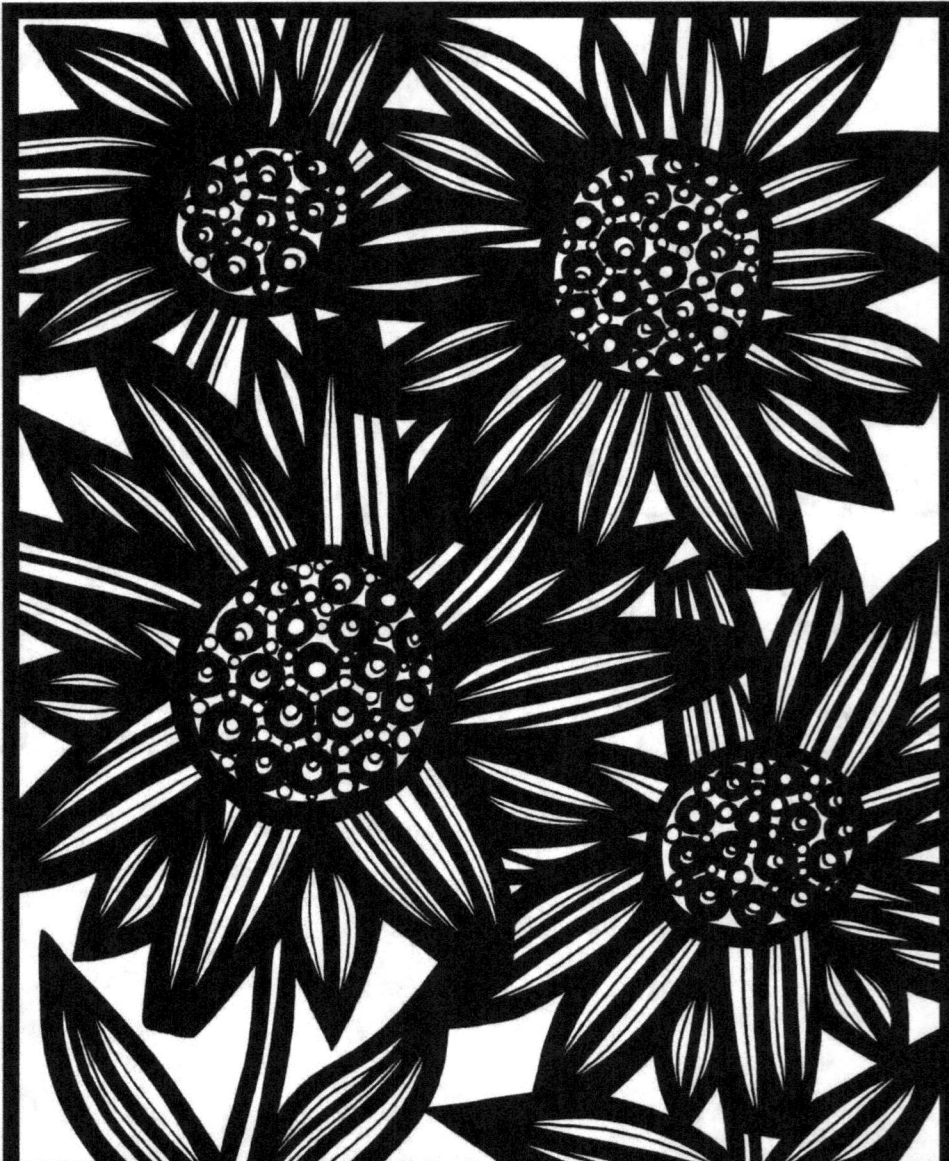

With his heart and soul,
Saint Francis was an alchemist.

With words,
lost in his work.

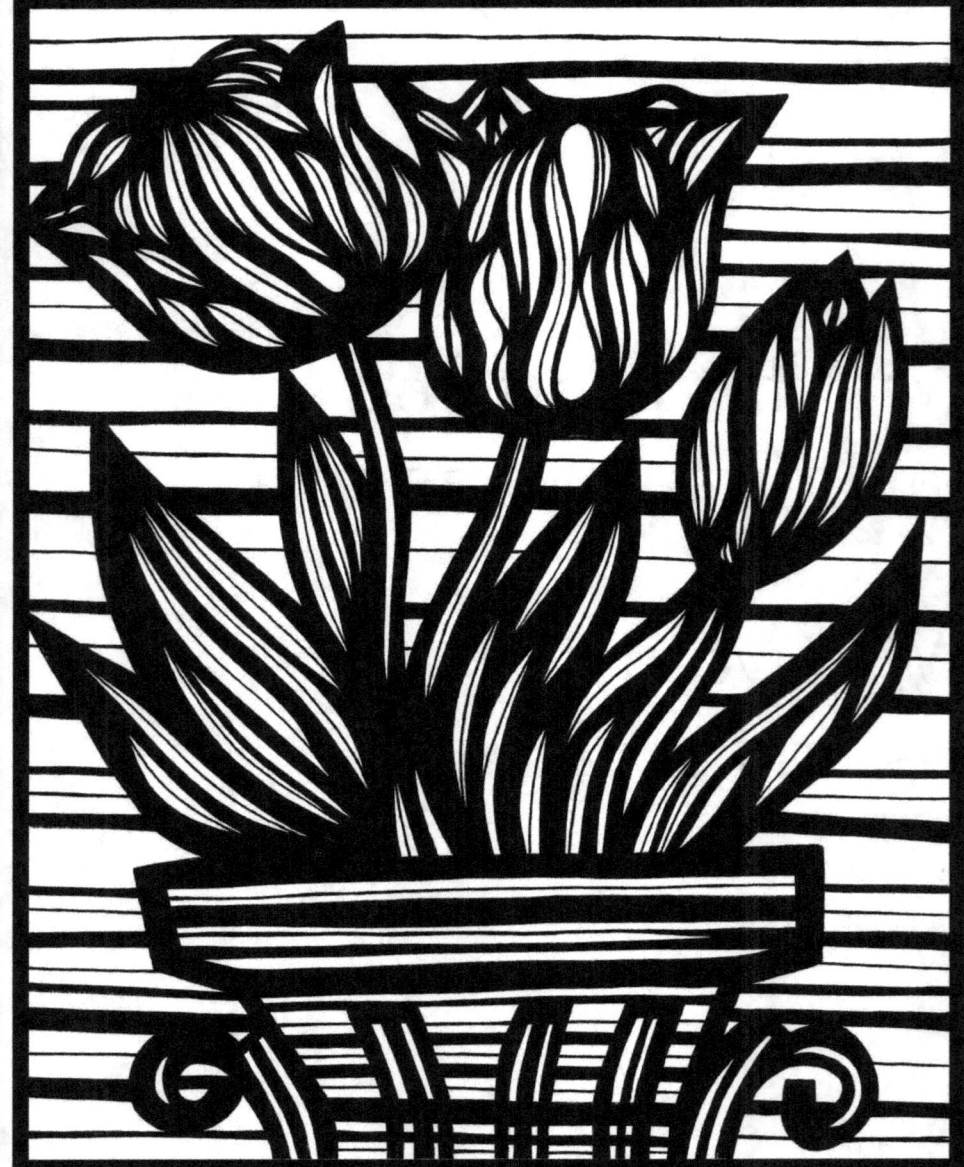

Bent in his toil,
his whole being helped,

To transform this world
for all centuries to come.

"Intentional Respect"

by

Zbigniew Zolkowski

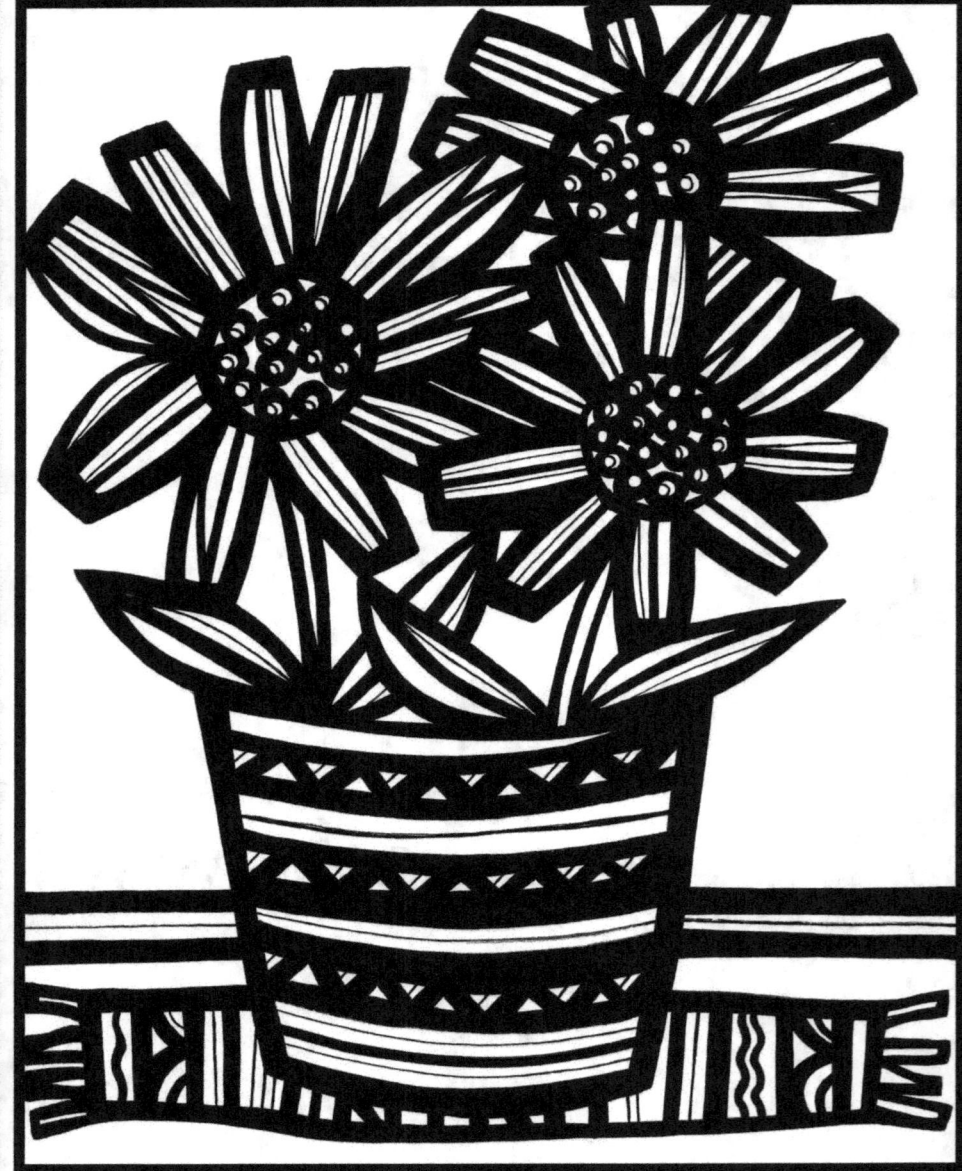

Flowers have
profound power
of divine
poetry and verse.

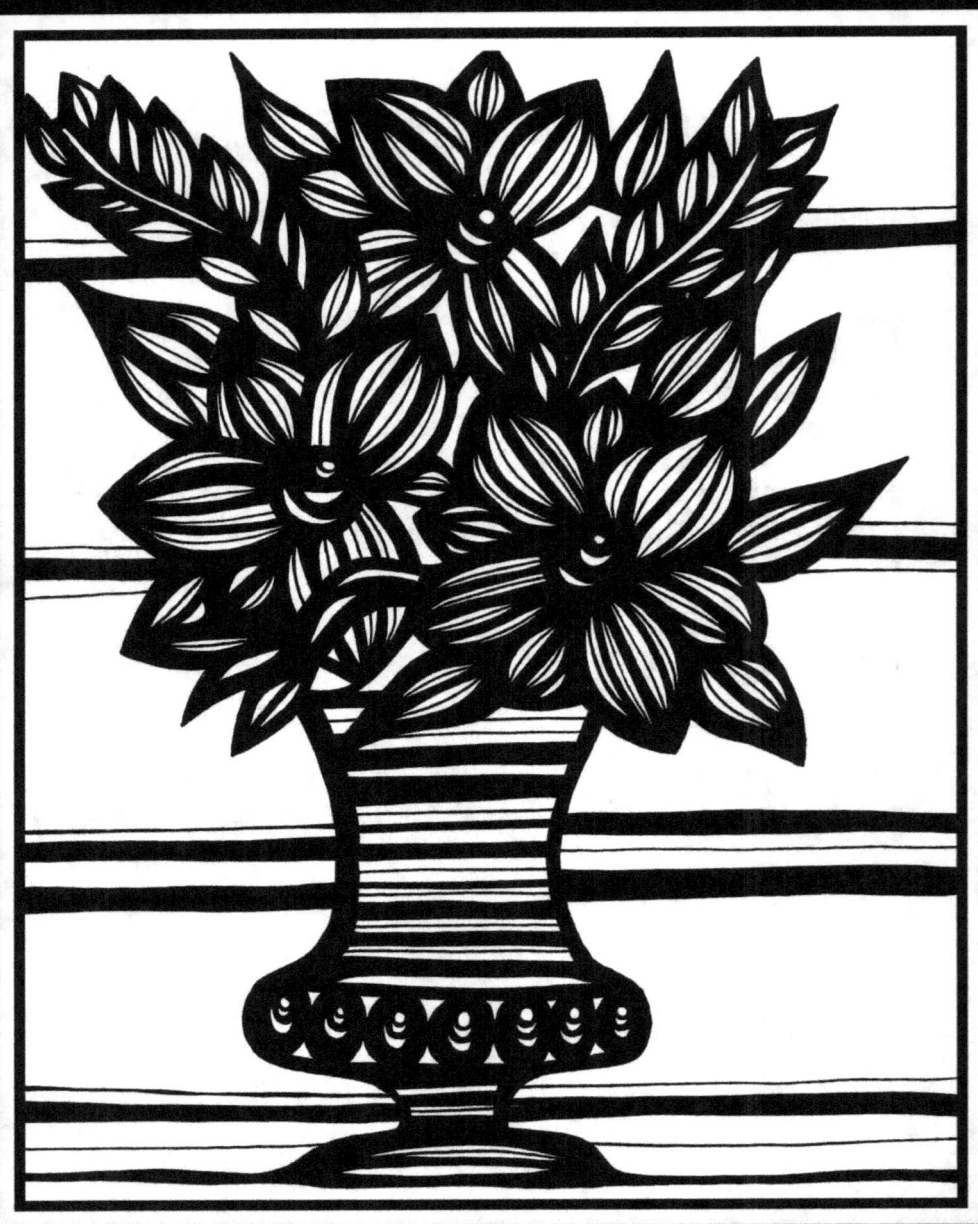

They have an
innate subtlety
of beauty and love.

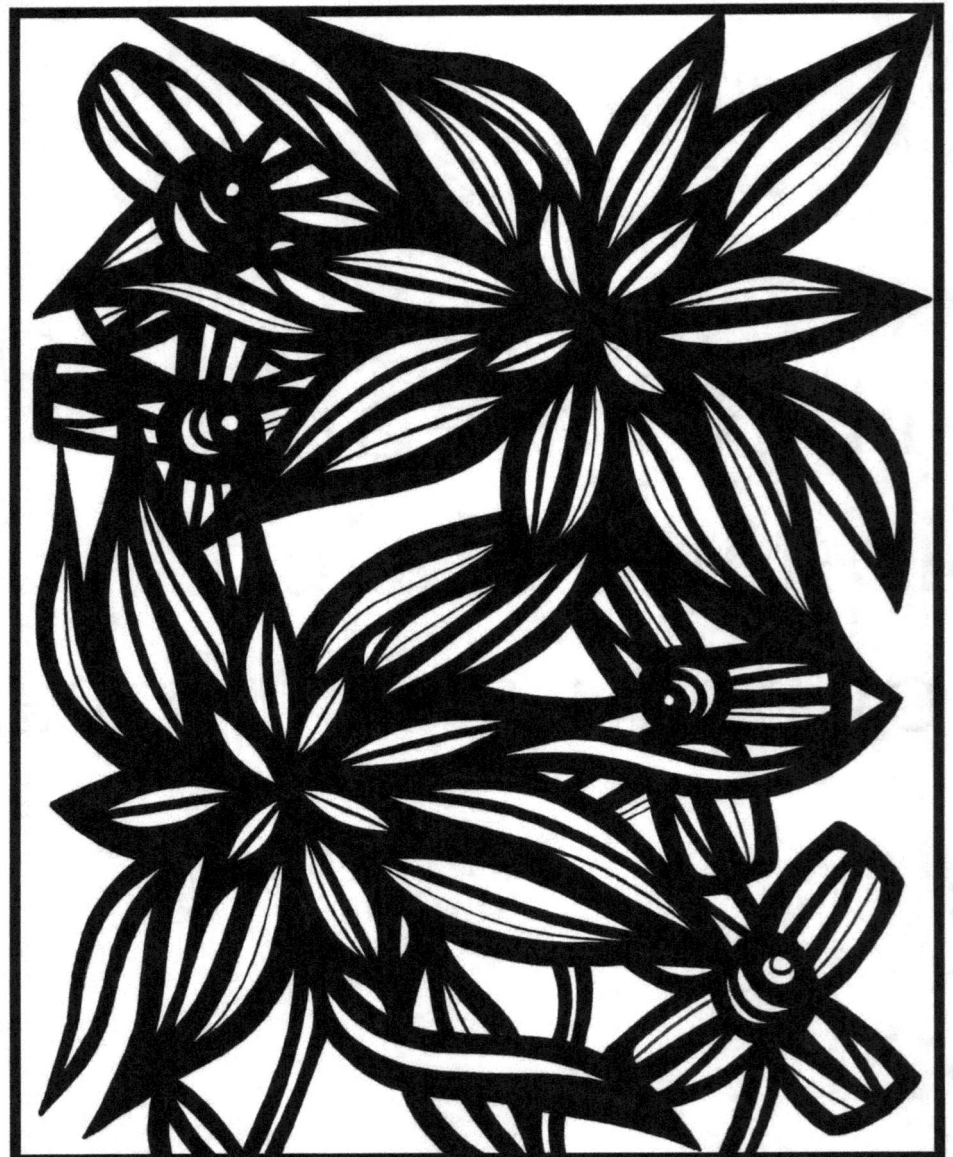

An attraction
that can transform
a heart of stone.

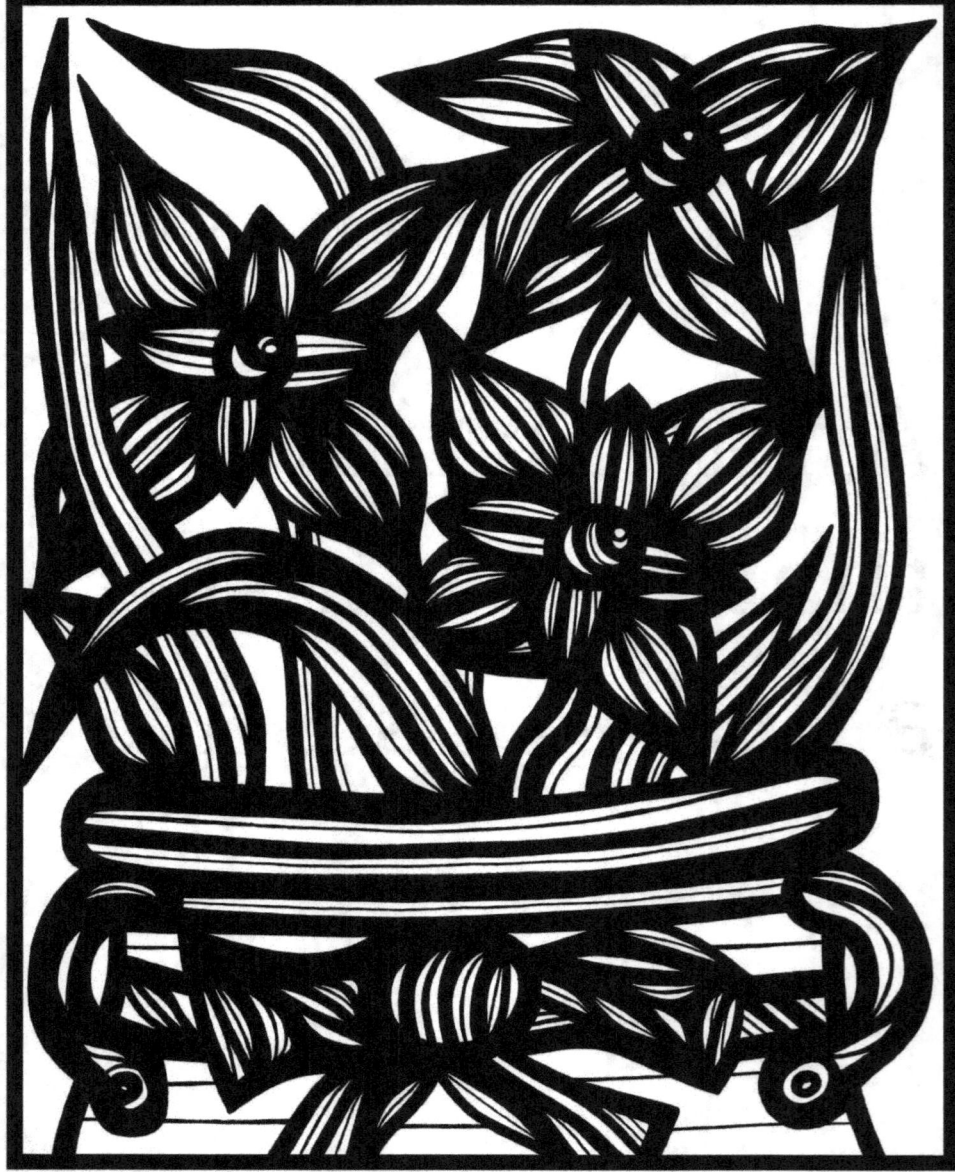

Flowers can
work miracles.

There is nothing
more lovely
then a beautiful bouquet.

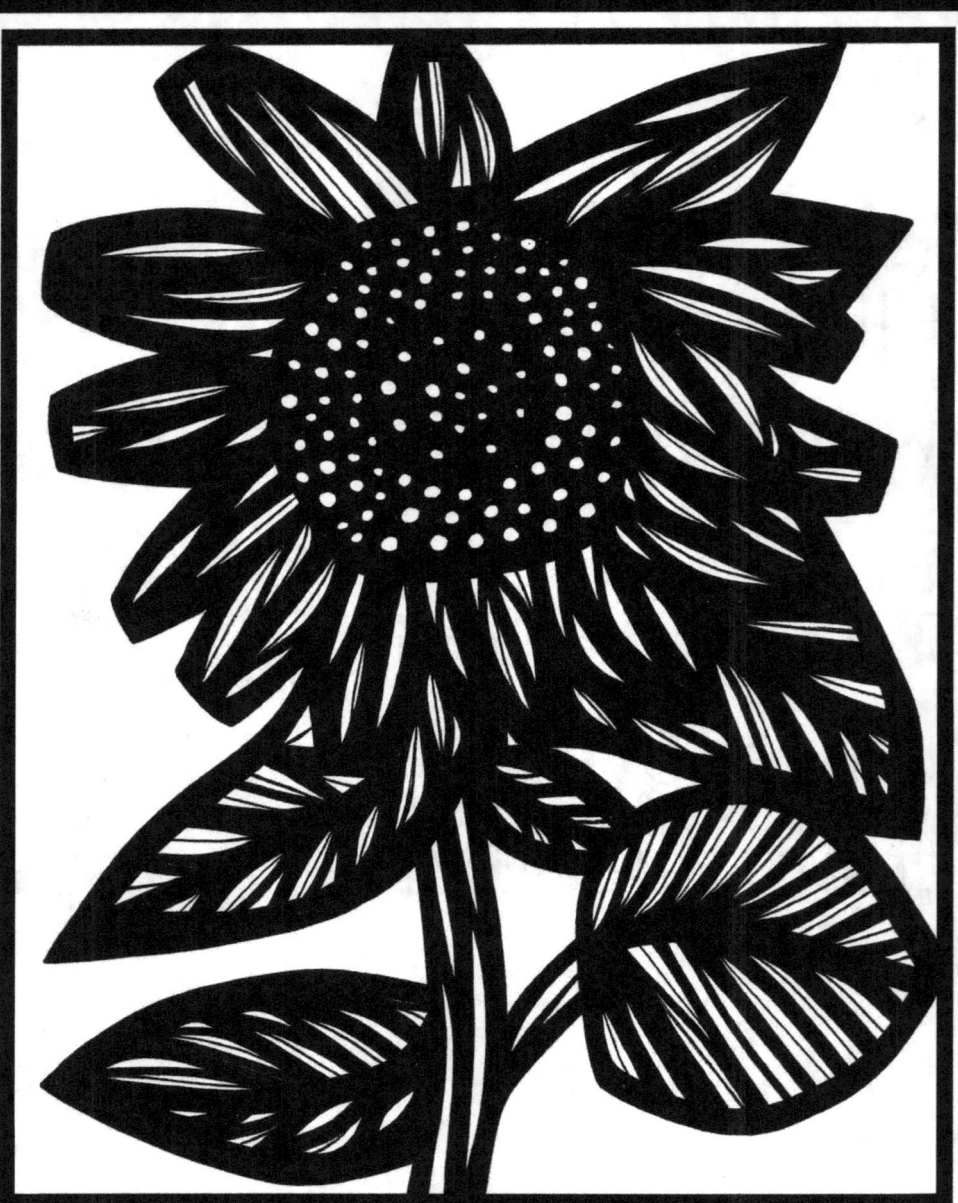

With intentional respect
for just one sunflower,

if placed on an altar
or hand can
change our world.

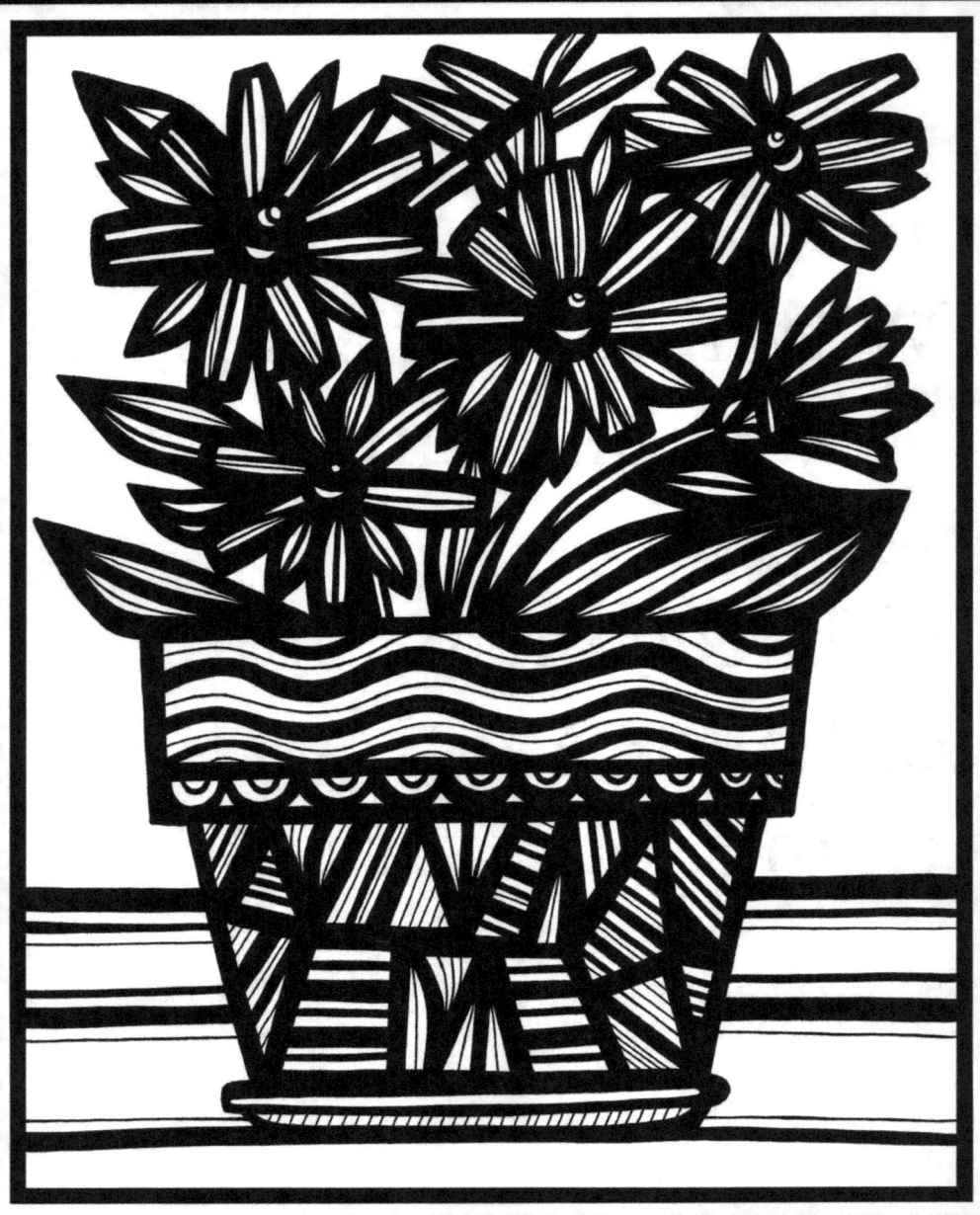

For the
best flowers
can make
war disappear.

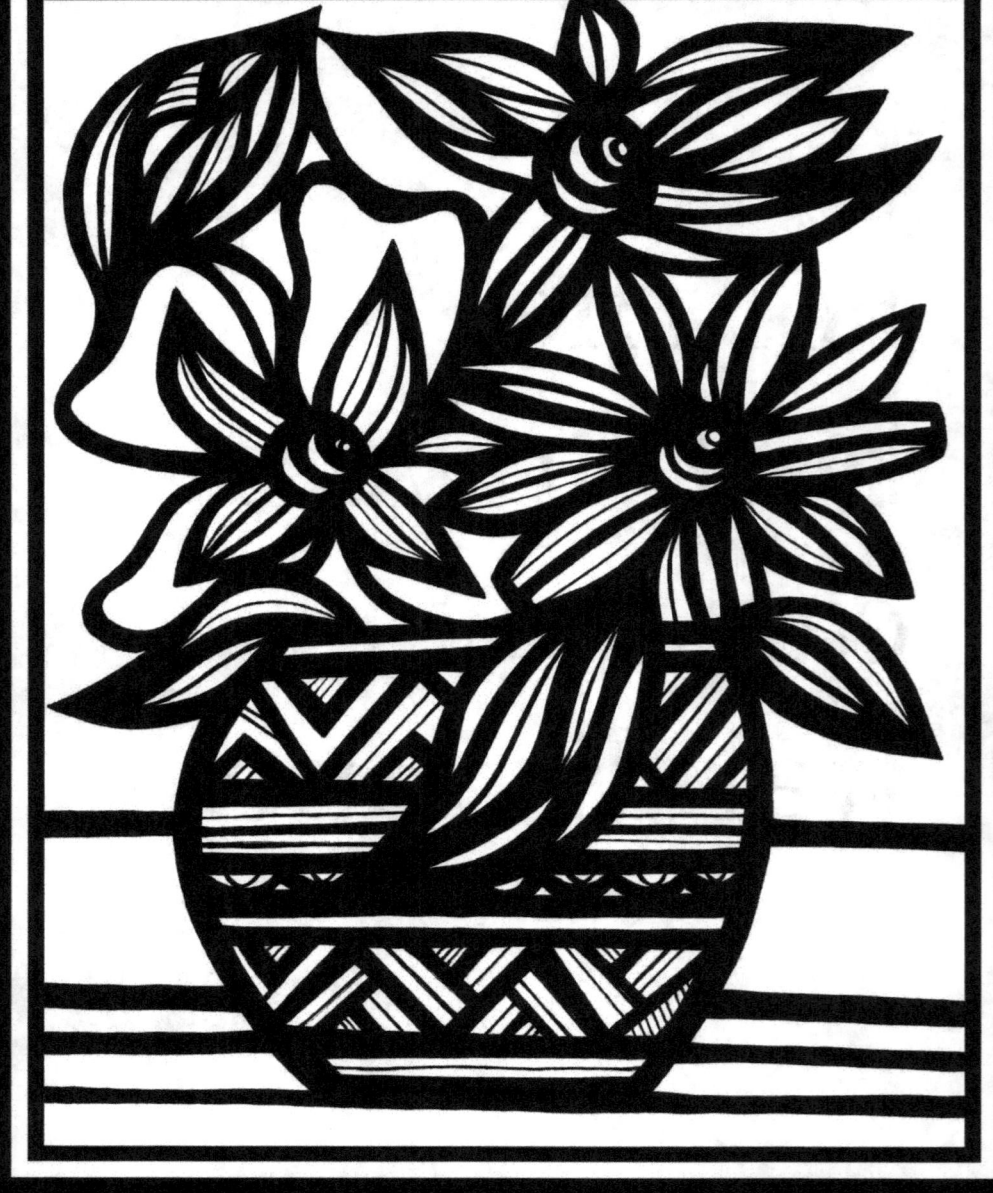

Flowers can mend our fear,

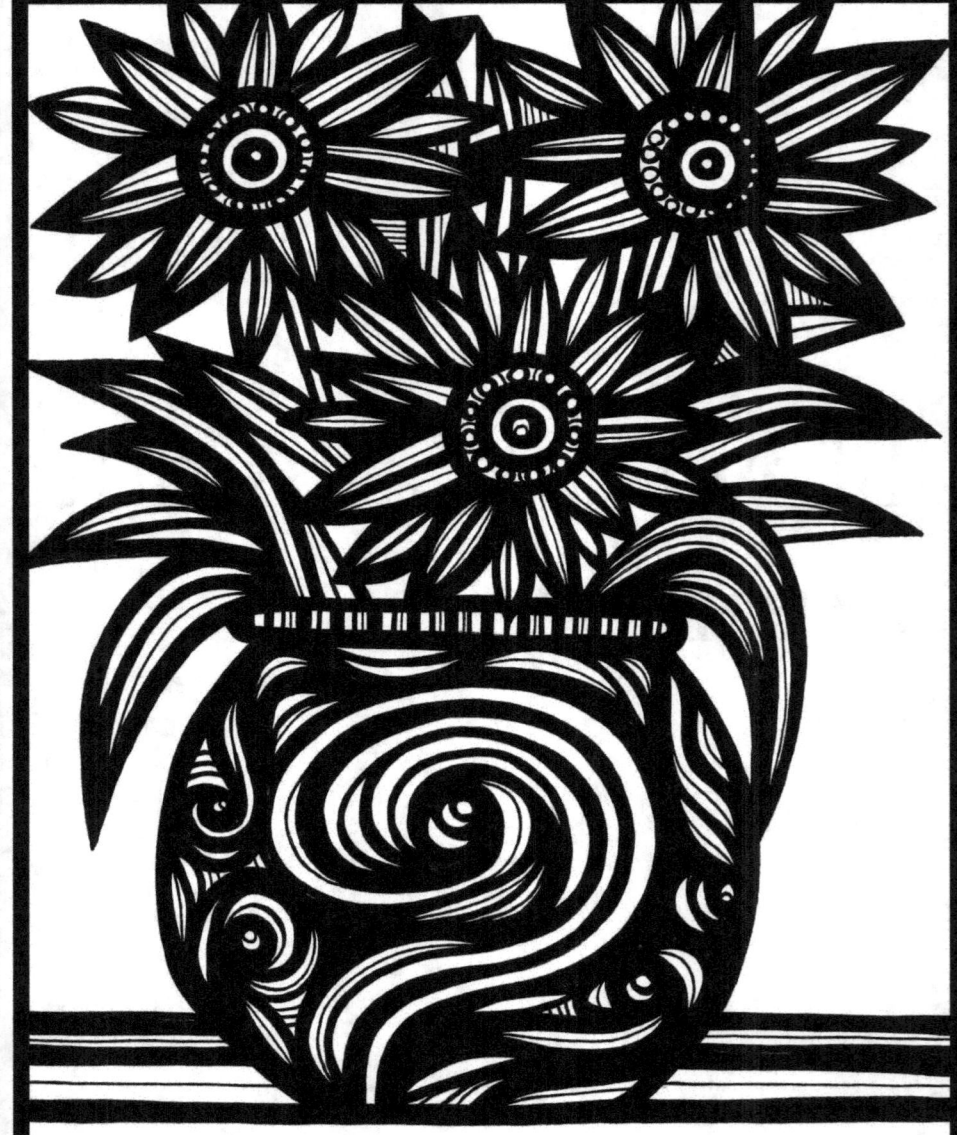

Flowers are
the ultimate
and most intimate,

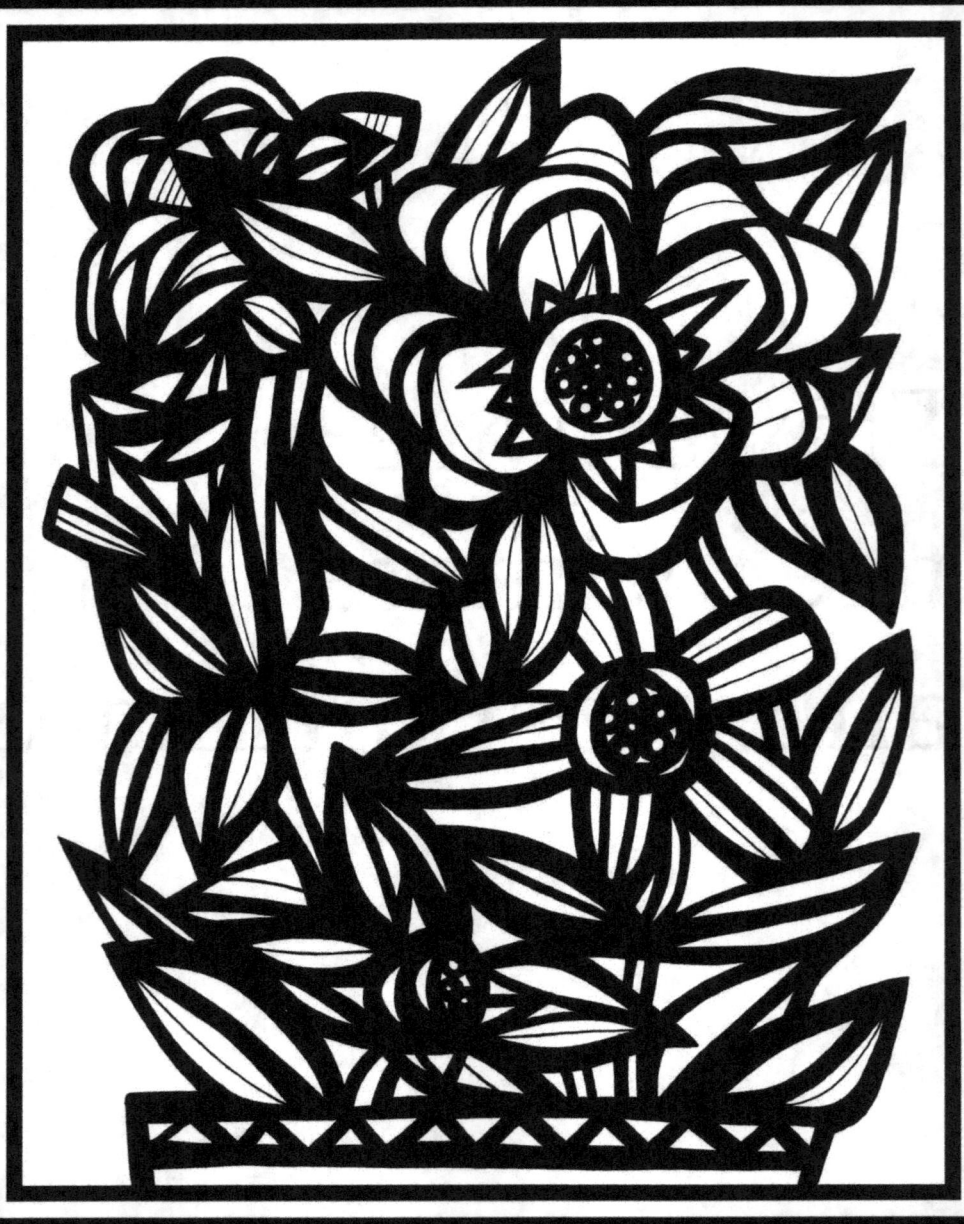

forms of
earthly prayers.

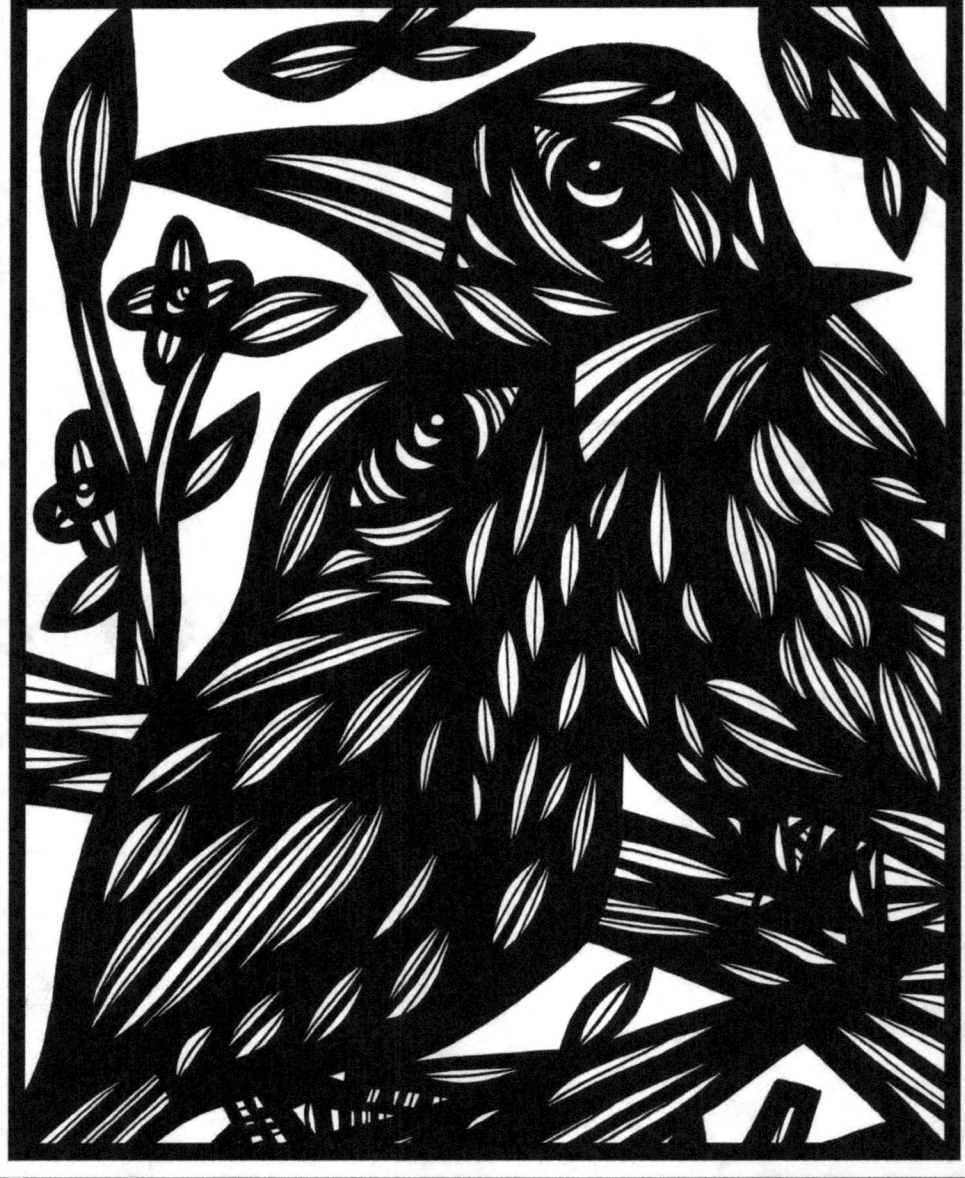

The Sail of the Season

by Eddie Alfaro

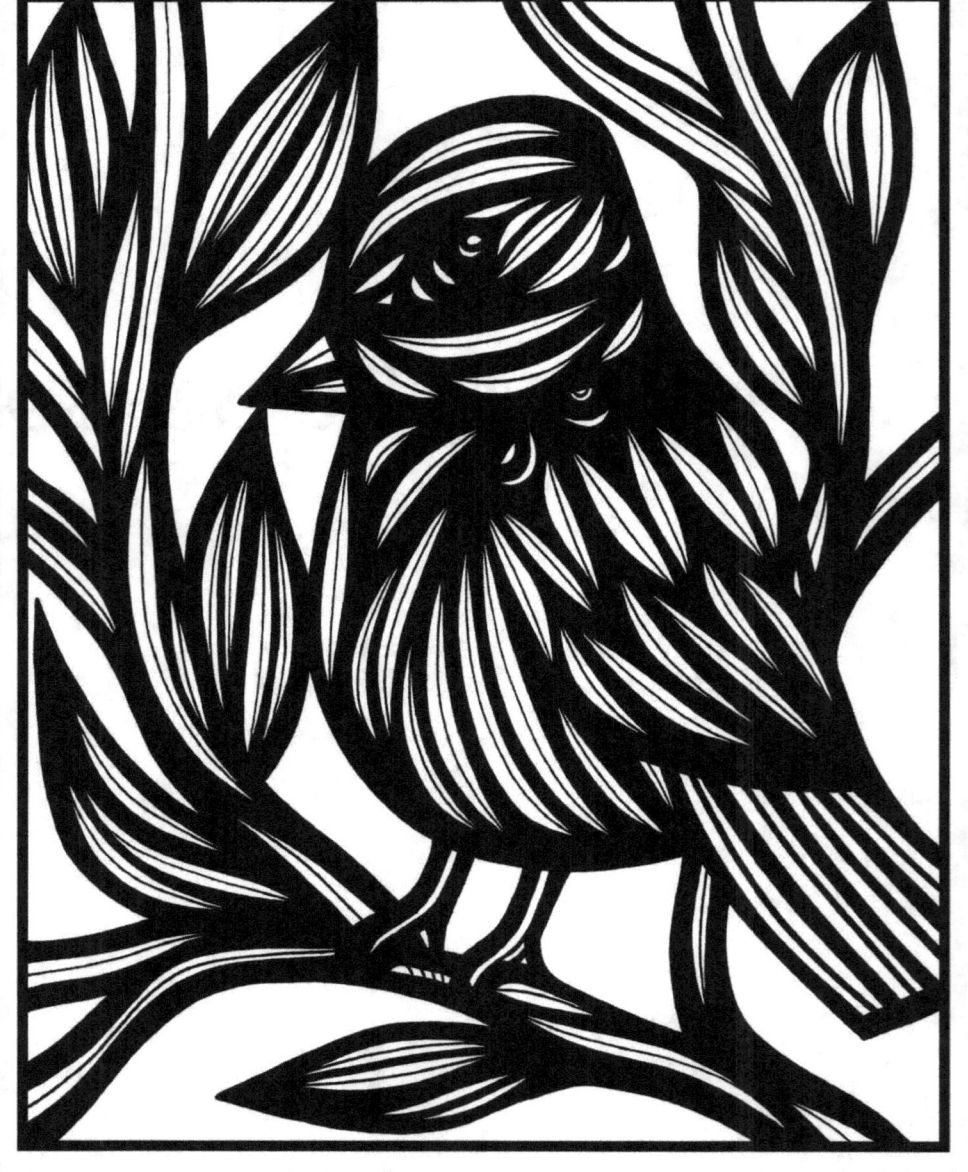

Bold in its initiative, relative to the size.

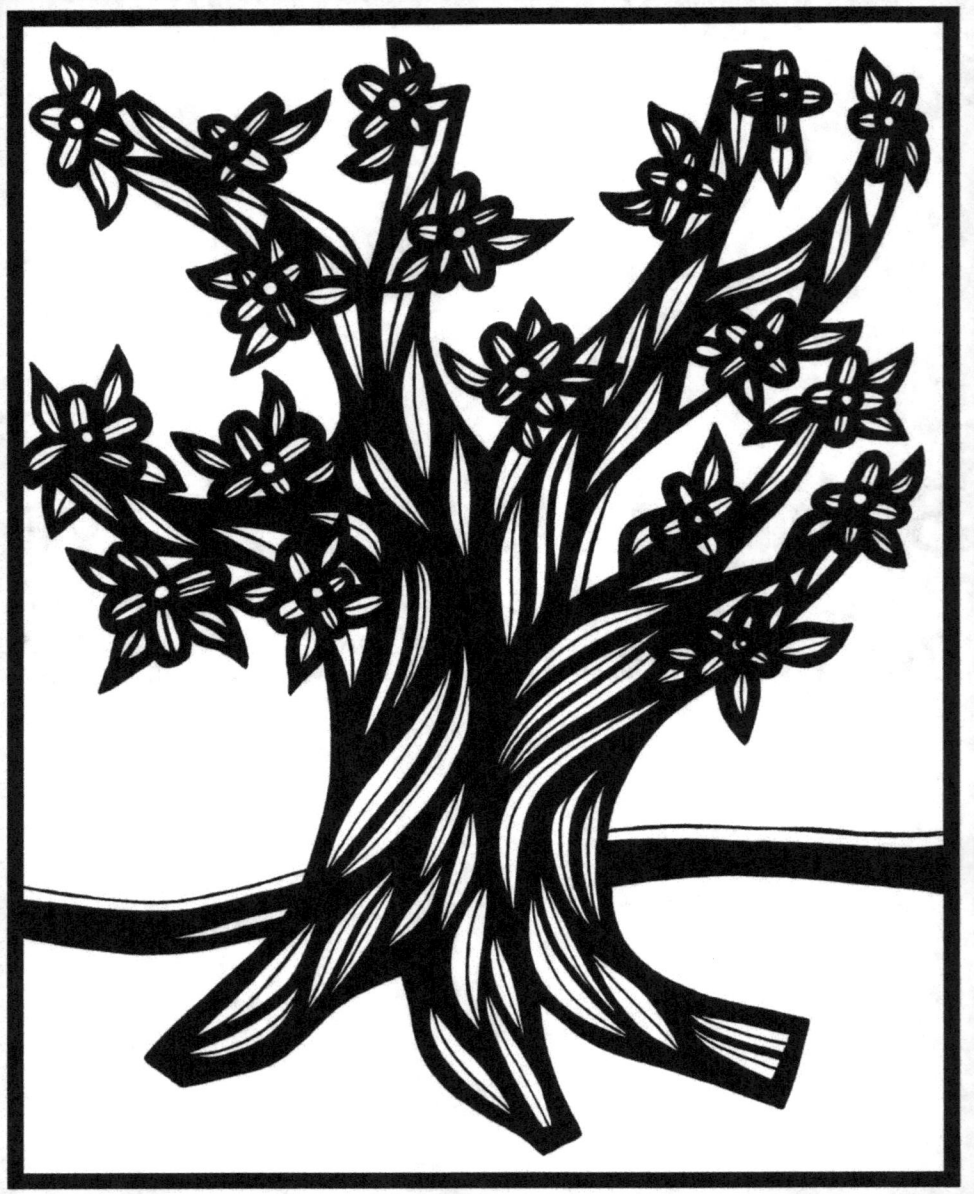

Signature of a natural born mention of a tree.

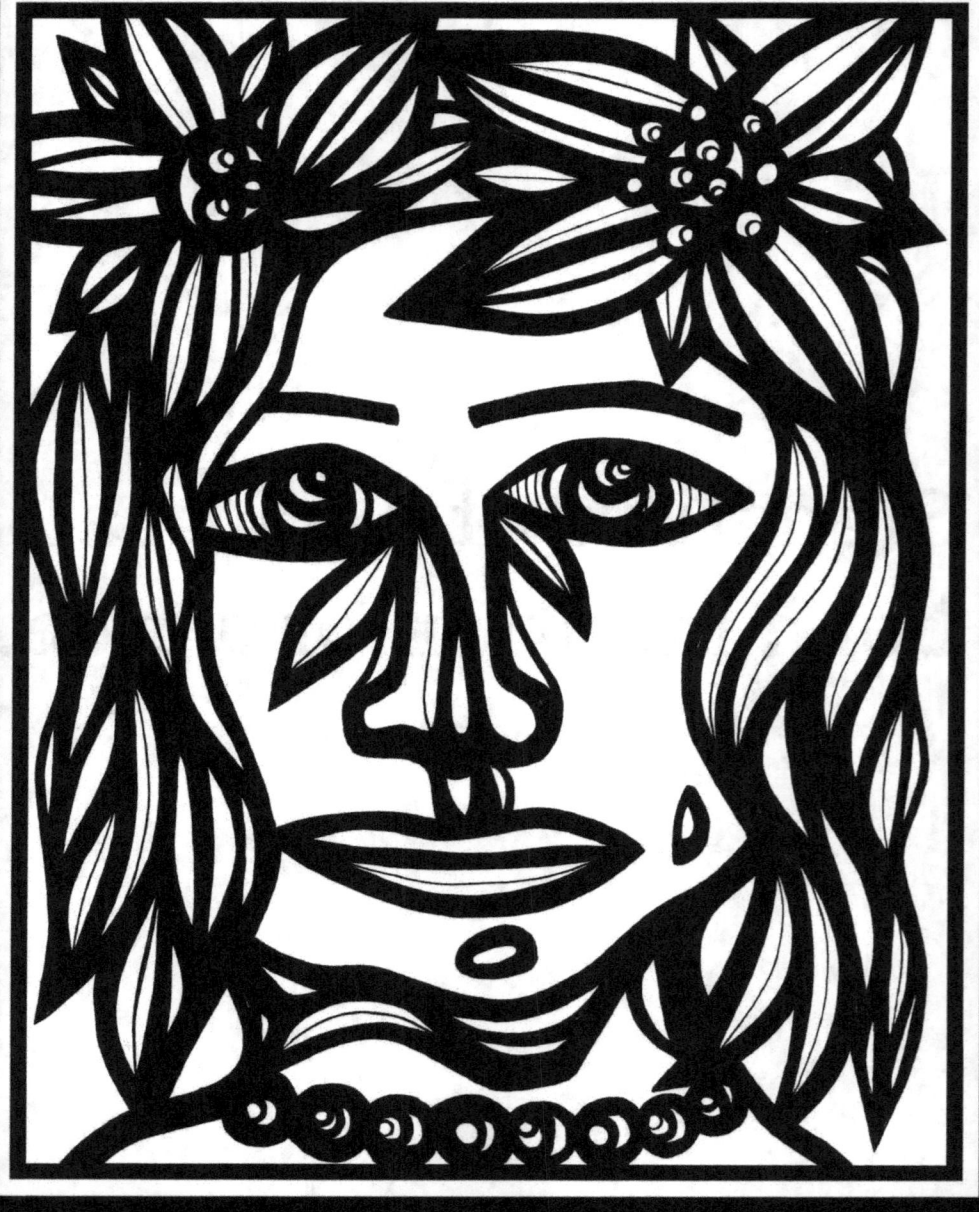

The golden sight that shows a turning key.

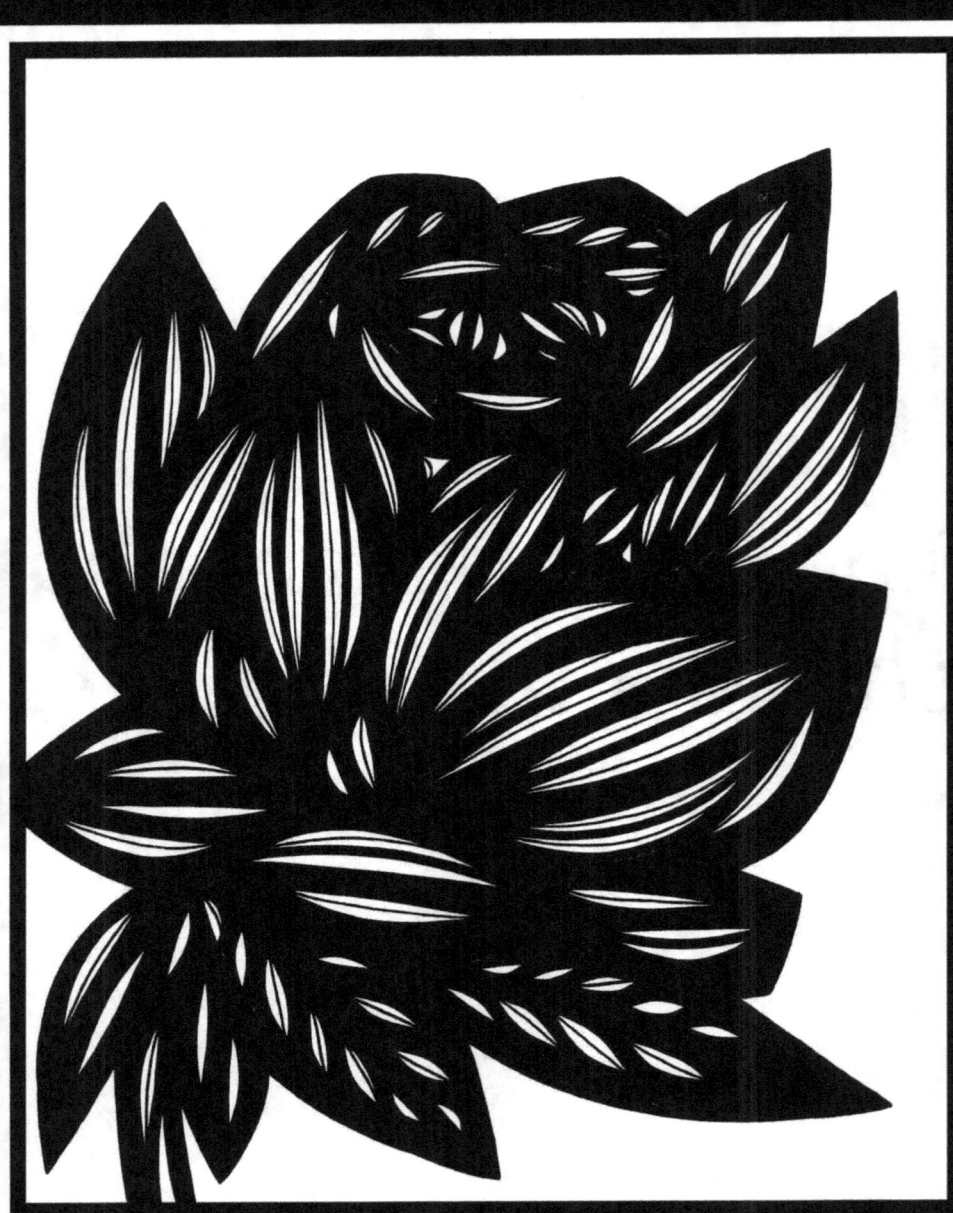

A reason to believe that something is becoming what it is.

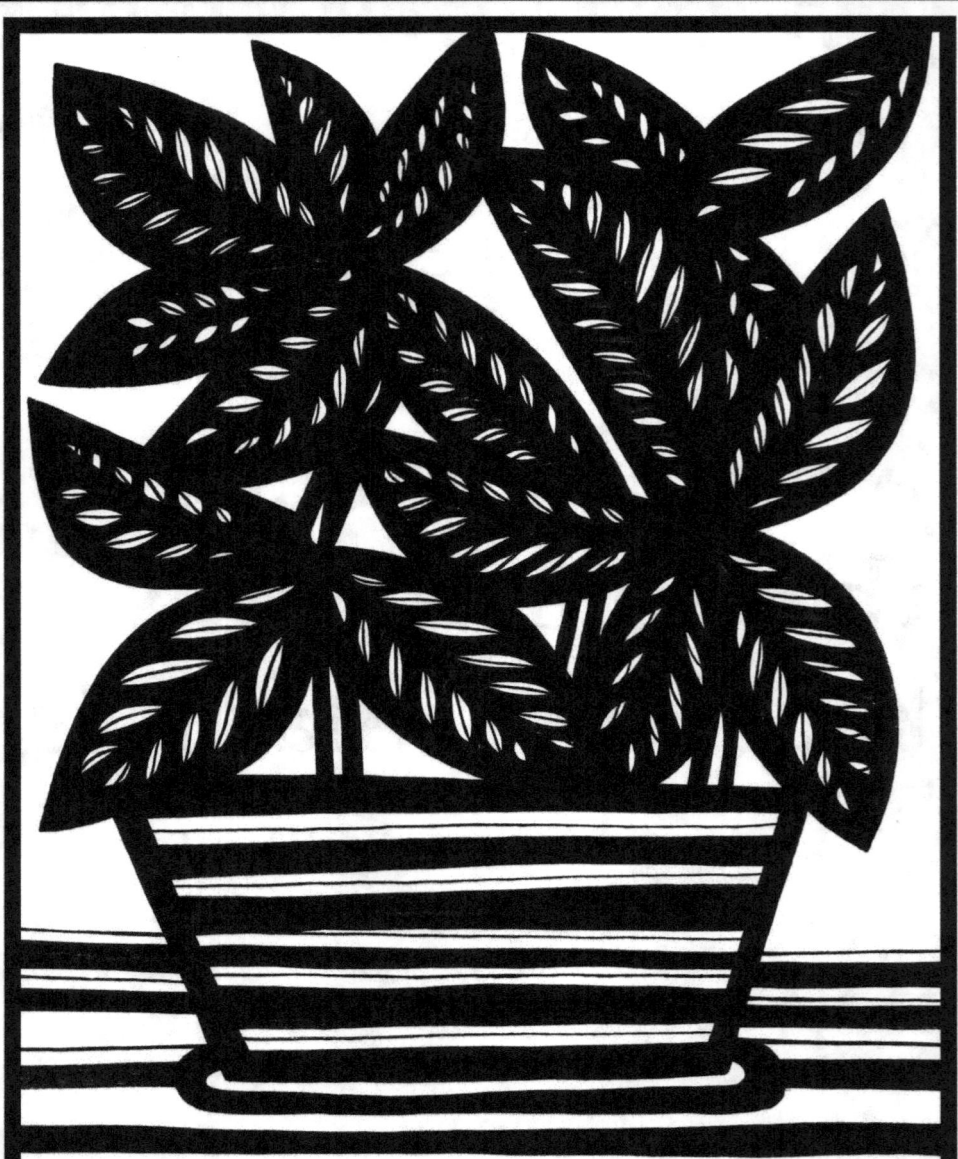

Future shown in the
past and present,
a system grace belongs
to a mechanism.

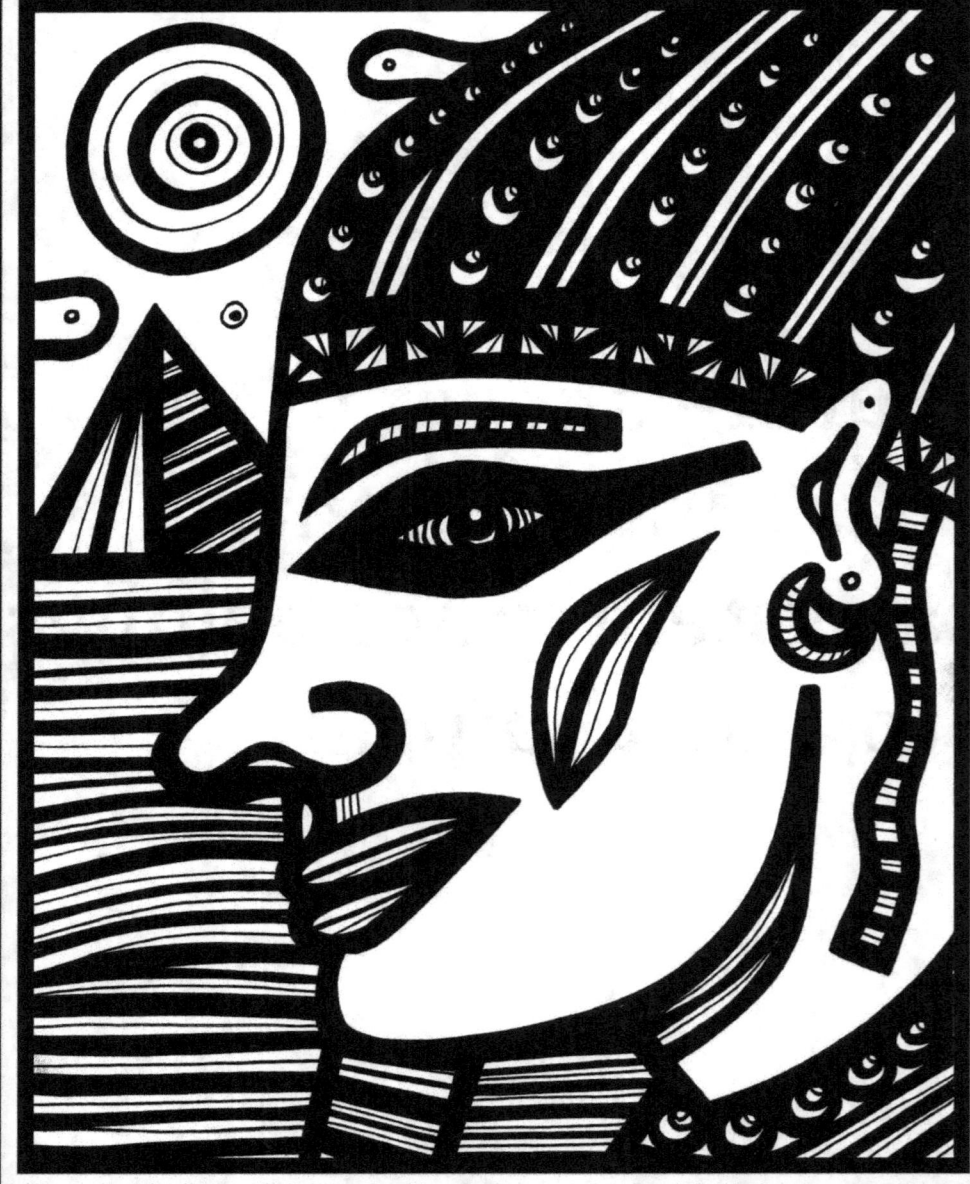

Seen in the mix
is a version of
the truth put through
the test of time.

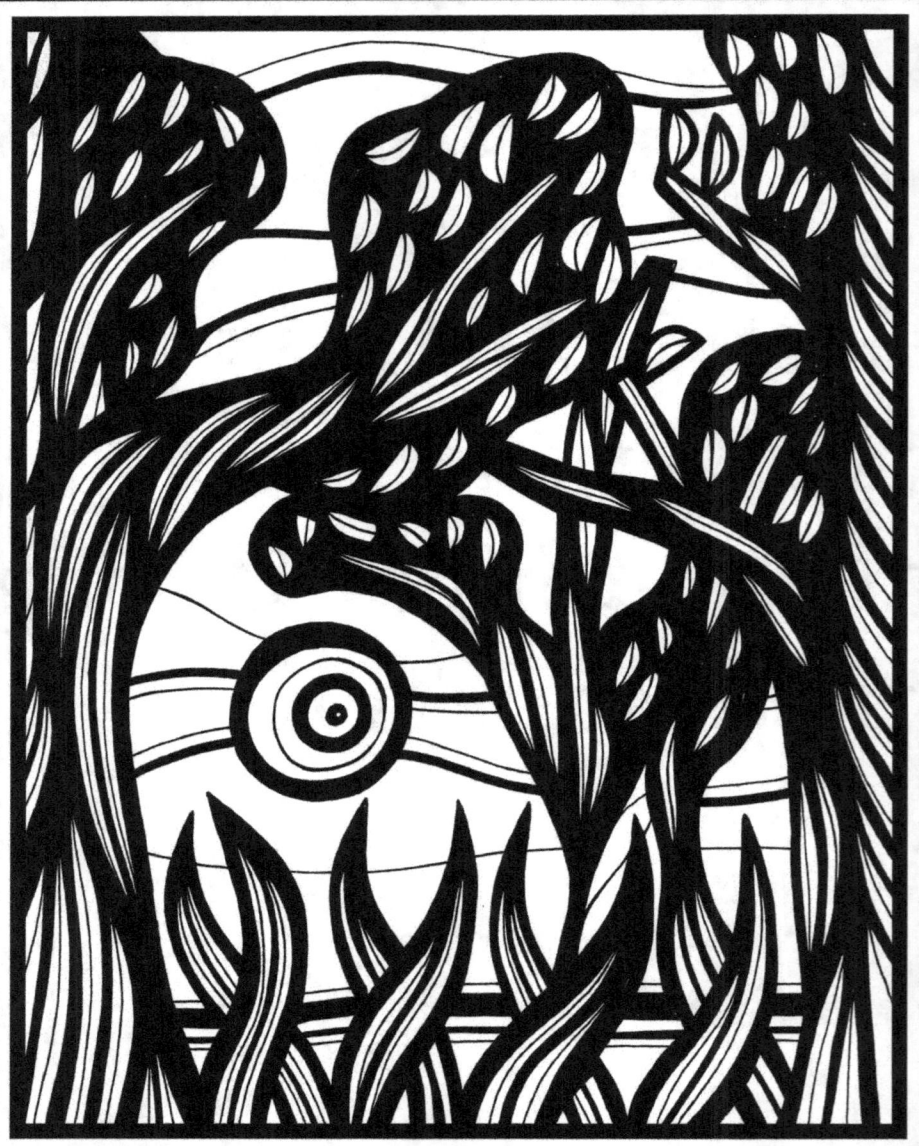

Precious is the experience of inner swirling sun storms.

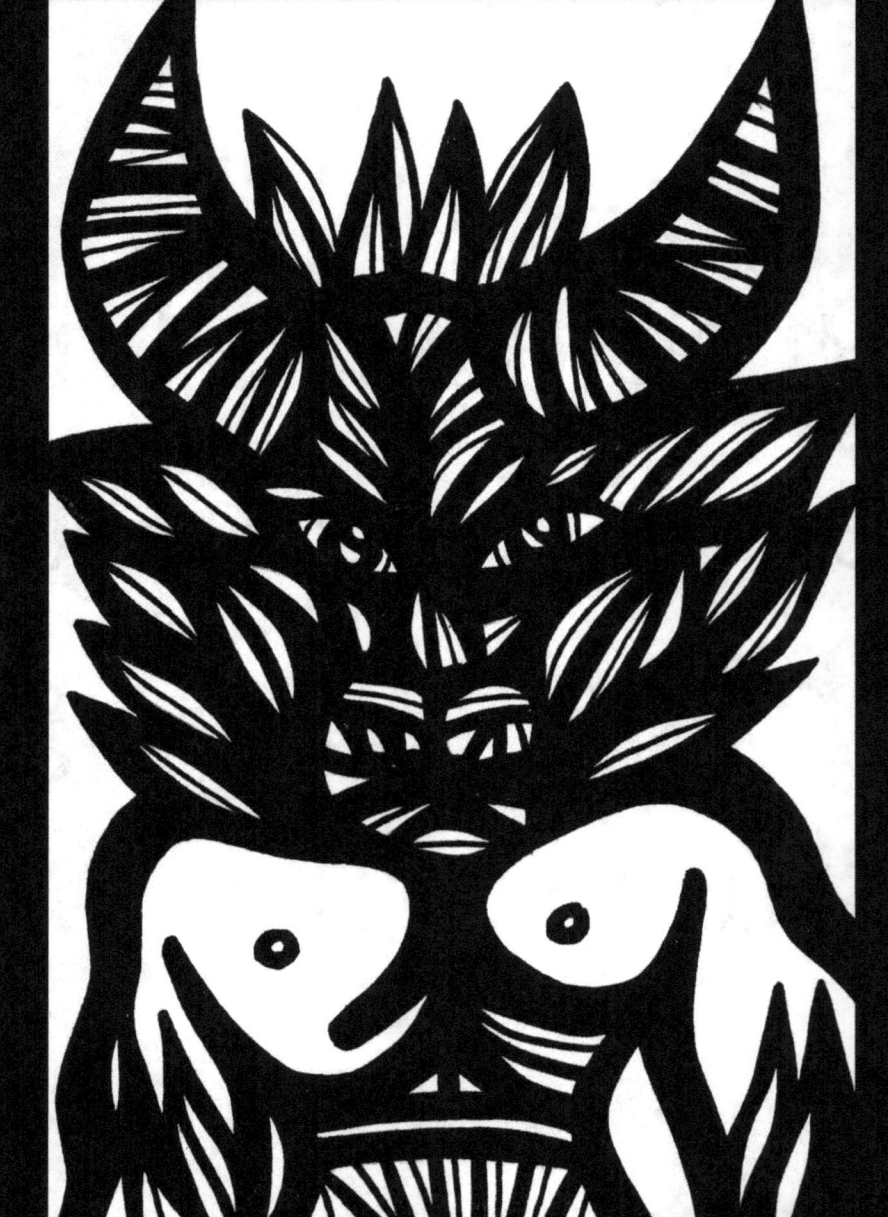

An energy that goes to the top from the bottom.

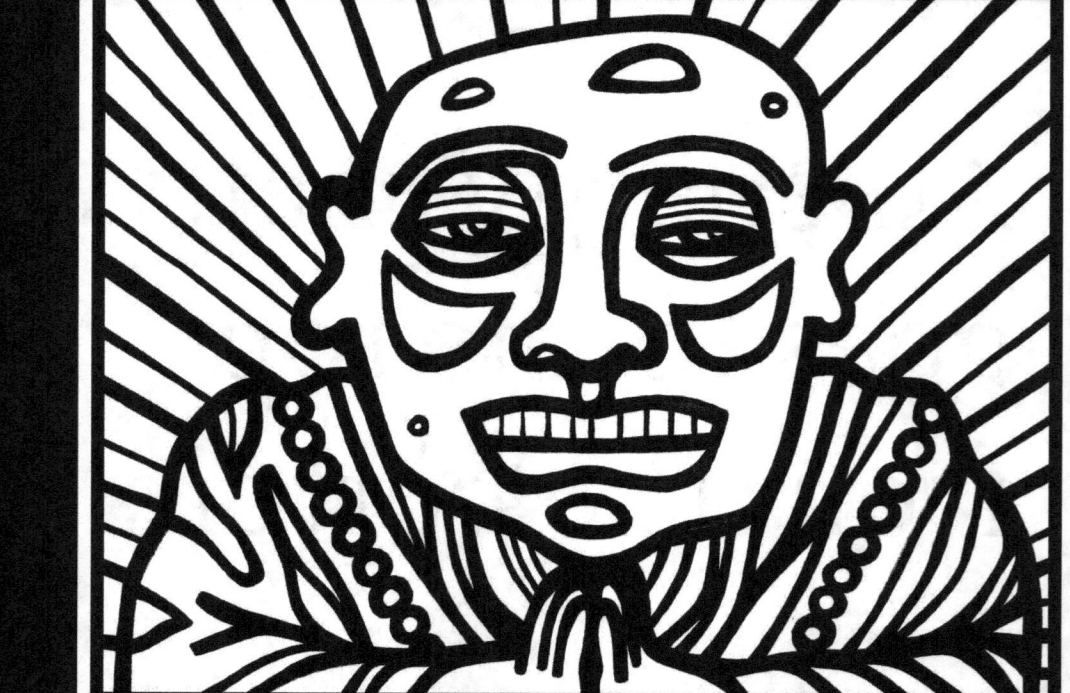

The form that shapes itself, from elements.

An event unexplained
that created life.

THE END

Words by:

Zbigniew Zolkowski

and

Eddie Alfaro

Artwork by:

Eddie Alfaro

www.ingramcontent.com/pod-product-compliance
Lightning Source LLC
Chambersburg PA
CBHW072305200526
45168CB00014B/839